Transforming
BIBLE STUDY

Understanding God's Word Like You've Never Read It Before

BOB GRAHMANN

IVP Connect

An imprint of InterVarsity Press
Downers Grove, Illinois

InterVarsity Press
P.O. Box 1400, Downers Grove, IL 60515-1426
World Wide Web: www.ivpress.com
E-mail: email@ivpress.com

InterVarsity Press® is the book-publishing division of InterVarsity Christian Fellowship/USA®, a movement of students and faculty active on campus at hundreds of universities, colleges and schools of nursing in the United States of America, and a member movement of the International Fellowship of Evangelical Students. For information about local and regional activities, write Public Relations Dept., InterVarsity Christian Fellowship/USA, 6400 Schroeder Rd., P.O. Box 7895, Madison, WI 53707-7895, or visit the IVCF website at <www.intervarsity.org>.

Chapter nine of this book appeared in slightly different form in the 2002 edition of ReFORM *Magazine.*

Cover design: Cindy Kiple
Cover image: couch: ©Giordano Aita /Depositphotos.com
man with book: ©Leah-Anne Thompson/Depositphotos.com

ISBN 978-0-8308-1123-6

Printed in the United States of America ∞

Library of Congress Cataloging-in-Publication Data

Grabmann, Bob, 1949-
    Transforming Bible study: understanding God's Word like you've
never read it before / Bob Grabmann.
        p. cm.
Includes bibliographical references and indexes.
    ISBN 0-8308-1123-0 (pbk.: alk. paper)
    1. Bible—Study and teaching. I. Title
BS600.3.G73 2003
220'.071—dc21

                                                            2003010916

P	20	19	18	17	16	15	14	13	12	11	10	9	8	7
Y	22	21	20	19	18	17	16	15	14					

To Patricia,
my wife, partner and best friend,
and to Julie, Steven, Alex and Paula

*"I have no greater joy
than to hear that my children
are walking in the truth"*
(3 John 4)

CONTENTS

ACKNOWLEDGMENTS

I would first like to thank my friend and mentor Barbara Boyd, who has had the strongest influence of all in encouraging me to love God's Word, study it and teach it with power. Her "Bible & Life" discipleship training program has affected more than ninety thousand students in North America over the course of four decades, and now it is changing students' lives all over the world. This book is in her honor.

I would like to thank three current or former InterVarsity staff who had a specific influence on chapters of this book. Lindsay Olesberg, who has worked with me for the past few years to develop the method of Bible study described in this book, had a greater effect on the content of this book than anyone else. Lindsay introduced me to the dynamic idea of empowering the learners in a Bible study by having them develop questions from the text that they then set about to answer. Many of the ideas in chapters three, five and six of this book came from collaborations with Lindsay in training staff and students. Curtis Chang developed his revolutionary "narrative weave" approach to Bible study as an InterVarsity staff and staff director in Boston in the late 1990s. Much of chapter six of this book is influenced by Curtis and our e-mail discussions about narrative weave. Sharon Conley took our ideas for "communal discovery Bible study" and created a colorful, helpful manual for the staff and students in the Southeast. I am indebted to her for her ideas on entering the text of Scripture that appear in chapter three.

I am grateful to InterVarsity Christian Fellowship for maintaining its historic value of deep, powerful and relevant inductive Bible study. This book is a humble attempt to live in the tradition of William Webster White, Jane Hollingsworth, Paul Byer, Barbara Boyd, Eric Miller and many others who developed the methods of inductive Bible study, brought them to InterVarsity, refined them over the years and influenced the lives of thousands. Chapter eight of this book is a tribute to Paul Byer and his manuscript method.

I am so grateful to InterVarsity's former president Steve Hayner for encouraging me to take leadership in Bible study in InterVarsity, to pursue further training in educational methods and to share what I was learning with InterVarsity staff.

Finally, I want to thank those who trained me in specific aspects of Bible study: Pastor Charles W. Krahe, who faithfully and powerfully preached the Word to his congregation Sunday after Sunday for the first twenty years of my life; Janet Luhrs Balajthy, Paul Kazim and Sara Ratichek, who trained me in Daily Discovery and manuscript study; John Seiders, Fred Neubert, Jean Duerbeck and Shannon Lamb, who worked with me in learning to train staff in North America and overseas; my mentors at Trinity Evangelical Divinity School, Drs. Perry Downs, Linda Cannell and Ted Ward, who modeled and taught me the power of Nonformal Education; and the thousands of InterVarsity and IFES staff and students in North America and around the world who taught me about Bible study through their responses and feedback to my teaching over the years. May they continue to love God's Word, feed themselves from it and train new generations to hear from God in the Scriptures.

INTRODUCTION

As with many passages of God's living Word, the title *Trans-forming Bible Study* has layers of meaning.

Bible study is transformational. Studying the Bible with an open, seeking attitude, guided by the Holy Spirit, not only gives knowledge, it deeply affects and changes not only an individual, but also groups, communities and cultures. The first two chapters of this book are about the power of God's Word to transform.

But the act of Bible study itself needs to be transformed. For the past twenty-four years I have been on staff with InterVarsity Christian Fellowship, an evangelical ministry among students that is active on about six hundred university campuses in the United States. InterVarsity is a member movement of the International Fellowship of Evangelical Students, a family of evangelical campus ministries at colleges and universities in more than 140 countries. InterVarsity has a long and proud history dating from the "Cambridge Seven" movement and revivals led by Dwight L. Moody in England in the late nineteenth century.

An important part of this heritage is a deep value of and emphasis on inductive Bible study. Inductive Bible study is to InterVarsity what the Big Mac is to McDonald's. It is one of InterVarsity's "signatures," what the organization is known for.

Inductive Bible study refers to studying the Bible "from the text out." It requires that one start with a close study of what the text of a passage actually says, then derive meaning, application and relevance from the text rather than read one's ideas or preconceptions into the text. Inductive study is vigorous, deep, serious Bible study, engaging the full faculties of the mind. But inductive Bible study is not simply an intellectual exercise. The Bible is God's living Word, and studying the Bible involves the whole person—heart, emotions and soul, as well as the mind. The goal of inductive Bible study is not just to learn things about the Bible, or even find the main points of a text (although this is essential to inductive Bible study), but to hear from the living God and obey him.

InterVarsity has provided some wonderful methods of inductive Bible study to generations of students, to the church and to the world of missions. Barbara Boyd's "Bible & Life" discipleship training program and Daily Discovery method of inductive Bible study, the late Paul Byer's manuscript method and InterVarsity's LifeGuides Bible study series have enriched thousands of students, laypeople, pastors and missionaries and helped them learn to love and study God's Word.

Now it is a new era. The "Millennials" have risen up to take the place of Generation X, the Me Generation and the Baby Boomers. This new generation has a different view of life, different values and ways of learning. In addition, postmodernism and its cultural aspects (called *postmodernity*) have influenced the worldview and lifestyles of contemporary students, even Christian students (see chapter two).

Because of these factors that affect us all, the method of Bible study itself needs to be transformed. The Bible *is* truth and it does have meaning—and that meaning can be discovered through careful, deep, inductive study of the text. We need to develop new ways to approach Bible study that affirm the Bible's relational and experiential aspects just as much as its intellectual dimension, for the purpose of studying God's living Word is not only to discover truth but to hear from God, obey him and get to know him better. Experience, community and narrative need to become important dimensions of our approach to Bible study along with rigorous intellectual study.

This book is a primer on inductive Bible study for a new generation. It derives from

- my experience teaching and training staff, laypeople and students around the world in Bible study for the past thirty-four years

- my research into the way this generation approaches the Bible

- the research, deliberations and recommendations of the InterVarsity Bible Study Task Force

- my collaboration with InterVarsity area director Lindsay Olesberg to develop a method of training eighteen hundred students to lead small group Bible studies at the Urbana 2000 Student Mission Convention

The purpose of the book is to show how to study the Bible in ways that engage the whole person and that are relevant to contemporary ways of thinking. While affirming the basic tenets of inductive thinking (observing and then deriving meaning from the observations), the book will attempt to weave new emphases such as experience, community, narrative and curiosity into the strong historical fabric of inductive Bible study. At the end of each chapter you'll find exercises you can do on your own or with your group to learn this method of study.

This book is written to help the new generation of Christians all over the world as they develop ways to transform Bible study so that it is powerful and relevant to their generation and future generations. We hope it will also be a help to laypeople, pastors and missionaries of any age.

The first chapter of the book will show the power of God's Word. Chapter two illustrates the importance and power of inductive Bible study. The next chapters describe in detail a method of inductive Bible study that is especially relevant today and give practical tips for implementing transforming Bible study. Chapter nine puts the method together and describes step by step how an individual can study a text of the Bible, discover its meaning and apply it to life. Chapter ten is a practical guide to leading a small group inductive Bible study.

This book is written for Christian believers who use a standard version of the Bible in their own language. Readers of this book do not have to know the original biblical languages of Greek and Hebrew to learn to study the Bible effectively. But they do need to love God's Word, seek to hear from God in his Word, and want to learn to study the Scriptures with power and depth so as to be transformed by God's Word.

1

THE POWER OF
GOD'S WORD

I went off to college searching for God. I had grown up in a
good church with an outstanding preacher, yet as a teenager I
was struggling. It was the late 1960s, the Vietnam War era, a
time marked by youth rebellion and searching. And I really was
searching. Early in my first year of college I made a friend
named Steve. We hung out, threw a softball around and studied
together; we became good friends. A few months into our
friendship Steve asked me if I would like to join an informal Bible study he was going to lead in his room. I was searching for
God, and Steve was my friend. How could I not go?

A small group of us met for four weeks and studied some passages in the Gospels about Jesus. At the end of the four weeks,
I realized deep in my heart what I had known in my head almost
all my life: that Jesus really did die for me and that he wanted
me to repent and turn to him. So I did, right in Steve's room, on
a warm May night in 1968. A combination of Steve's friendship,

my searching, my good background and the prompting of the Holy Spirit led me to Jesus. But actually it was the Spirit of God working through his Word, the Bible, that gave me life.

THE POWER OF GOD'S SPOKEN WORD

The phrase "word of God" has multiple meanings. First, it is God's spoken word—that is, what God literally speaks. From its first page, the Bible reveals a telling pattern. In Genesis 1, verses 3, 6, 9, 14, 20 and 24 start with the phrase "God *said*" (italics mine) and describe what God said. The repeated phrase "and it was so" follows God's speaking. The Genesis author (who I believe to be Moses) is showing that God *spoke* and the world came into being, God *spoke* and the oceans were created, God *spoke* and the stars and sun were made. The psalmist summarizes this in Psalm 33:6:

> By the word of the LORD the heavens were made,
>   and all their host by the breath of his mouth.

In other words, God's spoken word is his creative power.

In the summer of 1957 I was eight years old and staying in New York City with my Aunt Rita for a few days. One night she took me to a gigantic meeting in Madison Square Garden. Twenty thousand people were there. I also saw something I had never seen before in my eight years of life: a television camera! I sat there all night with my cheeks puffed out so that when I watched the show on television later I would recognize myself—the only kid in the Madison Square Garden crowd with his cheeks puffed out.

After some singers and some announcements, the main speaker got up. It was a young Billy Graham, in the midst of his now-famous New York City campaign. Forty-six years later, I still remember his sermon! He preached on Samson, explaining the gospel in simple but powerful terms by discussing the sins, repentance and forgiveness Samson experienced. God spoke through Billy Graham that night. What Graham said was not a new revelation or some secret knowledge. It was not the Word of God as the Bible is the Word of God. In fact, it was just a re-statement of the "old, old story" of the gospel. But God spoke!

At the end of his sermon, when Graham asked people to come forward to receive Jesus, my Aunt Rita took my hand and, with tears in her eyes, said, "Let's go down there." She died a year later. Only much later did I learn that Aunt Rita, who up to that time was a pretty secular person, was in the midst of a se-vere depression in 1957 and had gone to the Billy Graham meeting out of curiosity. She accepted Jesus and was trans-formed that night.

God, by his spoken word, brought the universe into being. And by his spoken word, through Billy Graham, he created eter-nal life in Aunt Rita.

THE POWER OF GOD'S INCARNATE WORD

God's spoken word is his creative power. Jesus is the powerful Word of God incarnate (that is, in the form of a person). John 1:1-5 echoes the Genesis 1 account but identifies God's word as a person. This Word was in the beginning with God, and in fact was and is God (vv. 1-2). All things were made through him, so he is the agent of creation (v. 3). Light and life are in him (vv. 4-5). In verse 14 John reveals who this Word is. He is the one who became flesh and dwelt among us, "full of grace and truth." This awesome, eternal Word of God, God himself, agent of creation, light and life, is Jesus. Jesus is God's powerful Word in a person.

As a staff person with the International Fellowship of Evangelical Students, I get to go all over the world and teach students how to study the Bible. I have been to rich countries, poor countries, free countries, communist countries, postcommunist countries, left-wing dictatorships, right-wing dictatorships and religious dictatorships. In all of these countries, I have encountered students who have come to Jesus, who know him, who love him, who want to serve him. Although these students differed in nationality, race, culture, economics, politics and upbringing, they were unified by a common bond—Jesus. In Jesus they all know God, for Jesus reveals God. That is what a word does—it reveals a meaning. Jesus is the Word of God because he reveals God. He brings us to God. In him we have the right to be called "children of God" (John 1:12). Jesus is the Word of God in a person. He reveals God to the world.

THE POWER OF GOD'S WRITTEN WORD

God's spoken word is his creative power, Jesus is his Word in a person, and the Bible is God's powerful Word written down. Not all parts of the church believe that the Bible is God's Word. Some say that the Bible is only a witness to God's word, or it becomes God's word only when it is preached, or only some parts of the Bible (usually the ones they agree with) are actually God's word. But this book rests on the conviction that the Bible is not just a witness to God's word but actually *is* God's Word.

There are many reasons for this conviction, too numerous to mention here. Booklets like John Stott's *The Authority of the Bible* (which is essential reading for any Christian interested in the Bible or Bible study) and books like J. I. Packer's *"Fundamentalism" and the Word of God,* R. C. Sproul's *Knowing Scripture,* Edward J. Young's *Thy Word Is Truth* or Kevin J. Vanhoozer's

Is There Meaning in This Text? help provide deeper insights into the Bible as the Word of God. The main reason for my conviction that the Bible is the Word of God is the teaching of the Bible about itself.

The Old Testament itself affirms that it is the Word of God with its many quotes of God's spoken words as recorded by Moses (Exodus 17:14; 34:1-7) and the prophets (Isaiah 8:1; 30:8; Jeremiah 30:2; Habakkuk 2:2). Paul makes this clear in the New Testament in 2 Timothy 3:16 when he says that "all scripture" (at the time, "all scripture" referred to the Old Testament, but now it includes the New Testament as well) is "inspired by God" (literally, "breathed" by God) and useful for teaching, reproving, correcting and training in righteousness. The Bible may be words on a page, little squiggles of ink on a piece of paper or dots on a computer screen, but in a wonderful, mysterious way those squiggles are God's written word, breathed by him.

Not only the Old Testament and the New Testament, but the center of the Bible, Jesus himself, affirms the inspiration of the Bible as God's Word. John Stott puts it best in *The Authority of the Bible:*

> What is the major reason why evangelical Christians believe that the Bible is God's Word written, inspired by his Spirit and authoritative over their lives? It is certainly not that we take a blind leap into the darkness and resolve to believe what we strongly suspect is incredible. Nor is it because the universal church consistently taught this for the first eighteen centuries of its life (though it did, and this long tradition is not to be lightly set aside). Nor is it because God's Word authenticates itself to us as we read it

today—by the majesty of its themes, by the unity of its message and by the power of its influence (though it does all this and more). No. The overriding reason for accepting the divine inspiration and authority of Scripture is plain loyalty to Jesus. . . . Jesus made several direct statements about the Old Testament's divine origin and permanent validity. He had not come to abolish the law and the prophets, he said in the Sermon on the Mount, but to fulfill them. Indeed, 'till heaven and earth pass away, not an *iota*, not a dot, will pass from the law until all is accomplished' (Matthew 5:17-18; cf. Luke 16:17). Again, 'Scripture cannot be broken' (John 10:35). . . . [Jesus] did not just talk about Scripture; he believed it and acted upon it himself. . . . This evidence cannot be gainsaid. Jesus endorsed the Old Testament as the Word of God. Both in his view of Scripture and in his use of Scripture he was entirely and reverently submissive to its authority as to the authority of God's own Word. (pp. 7, 9-10, 15-16)

The Bible is God's living Word (Hebrews 4:12). It is an ancient Word, written over the course of thousands of years in the languages and cultures of the ancient Near East. So we should use all the analytical and exegetical tools at our disposal to study it. But it is also a living Word through which God has spoken to people from ancient to modern times in order to reveal himself and show us how to know him, obey him and live. The Bible, as his living Word, is God's creative power. It is the sword of the Spirit (Ephesians 6:17). God uses his written Word to bring people to himself, to give them new life and a new birth (1 Peter 1:23). He uses his written Word to transform.

THE WORST BIBLE STUDY EVER

I began this chapter with the story of my conversion as a freshman in college, showing how God's Word had brought me to him. By the next year I had joined the Christian fellowship on our campus and was growing in Christ. Some of the guys in the fellowship challenged me to lead a Bible study for seekers just like the one I had been in with Steve. "No way!" I said. By that time I had felt a call to go to seminary and be a Christian pastor. "See me in six years, guys, after I have graduated from college, gone to seminary and learned Greek, Hebrew, theology, and church history. *Then* I will be able to lead a Bible study."

But my friends were persistent. Through their prayers and badgering, I came to realize one of the truths on which this book is based: one does not have to be a Hebrew and Greek scholar or a professional minister to be able to study the Bible and lead others in Bible study. It *does* take preparation, prayer and the community of God's people for help and support. But it doesn't take a professional. So after much prayer and with much fear, I decided that rather than wait six years, I would gather some of my friends and lead the study right then, as a nineteen-year-old student, just as Steve had done with me.

That first evening was the worst Bible study ever. I asked the guys on my floor if they would come, but I did it in such an ineffective way that only one guy showed up, and I think he came out of pity. I was nervous. I was sick. I was shaking. But I did lead the Bible study, just for that one fellow. At the end of the four weeks, I asked him what he thought, expecting to hear an honest assessment that this was indeed the worst Bible study in the history of Christendom. But instead he said, to my amazement, "I want to accept Jesus." I was shocked! I was amazed! I saw again the power of God's Word to bring new life, to transform. First I saw God transform me through his written word; then I saw him transform my friend.

The next year my Christian roommate and I led another study. We were third-year students by then, and we purposely lived on a floor with all first-year guys. We were old. We were bold. We were pumped by the power of God's Word. So we stood up the first night of school and said, "Listen, you guys. We are juniors, in our third year. You are freshmen, in your first year. *On this floor we do Bible study.* You *will* show up next Sunday night." And fifteen of them came! Many of them came to Christ or renewed their faith in him. He used his written Word to transform them and us, individually and as a group. God's written Word, the Bible, has the same transforming, life-giving power as his spoken word and his incarnate Word.

FULL OF SURPRISES

God's Word is also full of surprises. Young people who have grown up in churches sometimes think that the Bible is a boring book. They have heard its stories since childhood. The Bible has sometimes been used as a sledgehammer to force them to be good. But the Bible was "breathed" into being by a God who says,

> I am about to do a new thing;
> now it springs forth, do you not perceive it?
> I will make a way in the wilderness and rivers in the desert.
> (Isaiah 43:19)

God is *immutable:* he never changes in his essence, yet he seems always to be doing new things and surprising us with his grace and power. He constantly challenges our "conventional wisdom" through the Bible. For instance, many people think, based on a shallow reading of the Bible or what they have heard

22

or assumed, that the God of the Old Testament is a mean old judge and the God of the New Testament is a nice old fellow who is full of love. Yet, throughout the Old Testament, God is described as a God of "steadfast love" and "faithfulness." In fact, one of the strongest images for God in the Old Testament is of a wounded, loving, faithful spouse seeking to bring back his lost love. That is what the Old Testament book of Hosea is about.

In contrast, in the New Testament Jesus had a lot of tough things to say about judgment and hell. John the Baptist said of Jesus, "His winnowing-fork is in his hand, to clear his threshing-floor and to gather the wheat into his granary; but the chaff he will burn with unquenchable fire" (Luke 3:17). Not exactly a nice old grandfather sitting in his rocking chair hoping everyone on earth will get along.

The teachings of Jesus in the New Testament really set conventional wisdom on its ear. According to Jesus,

- we win by losing (Matthew 10:39).
- we live by dying (Matthew 10:39; John 12:24).
- we get by giving (Luke 6:38).
- we lead by serving (Matthew 20:26).
- we get to be first by being last (Mark 10:31).
- we defeat our enemies by loving them (Luke 6:27-31; Romans 12:20).
- we are responsible to initiate reconciliation with people when they offend us (Matthew 18:15), and we are also responsible to initiate reconciliation when we offend them (Matthew 5:23-24). So whether we are the offended party or the offender, it is up to us not to wait for others to come to us, but to go to them to initiate reconciliation.

- we are obliged to care about and spend time with sinners and outcasts rather than trying to curry favor with the rich, powerful and influential (Mark 1—4).

This is radical teaching. Jesus took almost every conventional thought of his day, and our day, and turned it upside down.

That is what the Bible is—a living Word, an exciting Word, a surprising Word, a Word from God, the Word of God. No wonder studying it and living it out is such a transforming experience. The following chapters will help us learn how to study God's powerful Word, so that we can be transformed by it.

INDIVIDUAL OR GROUP EXERCISES

1. From the examples in this chapter, you can see that I came to Christ through an "evangelistic Bible study," a Bible study for people who are not necessarily converted Christians but who are interested in learning what the Bible has to say. I then led evangelistic Bible studies for my friends and saw God work to bring people to himself through his Word.

   Evangelistic Bible studies are a very powerful way to share the gospel with friends. You can use the principles in this book, especially chapter ten, to lead an effective Bible study for your friends, even if they are not committed Christians.

   InterVarsity Christian Fellowship has a number of resources to help you set up and lead an evangelistic Bible study, and even some sample study outlines to use, on its website <www.ivcf.org>. InterVarsity calls evangelistic Bible studies GIGs—"Groups Investigating God." InterVarsity Press also has a number of resources for leading GIGs. See the IVP website at <www.ivpress.com>.

   Gather some friends who are seeking God and lead them in a simple Bible study for a few weeks. Use the principles in this book and the resources at <www.intervarsity.org> to prepare and lead your study. Get people to pray for you and your group. Watch how God works in their lives through his Word!

2. Think of a time when, as you were reading or studying the Bible, God called you to change something in your life or to obey him in some new way. What did you do? What was the result? How did it affect your life?

3. Ask your mentor, pastor, campus staff person or people in your church to share how they have been transformed by God's Word. If you are in a small group, collect these stories and share them together.

4. Individually or as a group, read some of the stories of people who have been transformed by God's Word. The biographies of people like Charles Colson, former counselor to the president of the United States and the founder of Prison Fellowship; Fanny J. Crosby, the writer of hundreds of inspiring hymns who was born blind; Dawson Trotman, founder of the Navigators; Bill Bright, founder of Campus Crusade for Christ; Billy Graham; Hudson Taylor, the great missionary to China; martyred missionary Jim Elliot; Dr. Martin Luther King Jr.; Mother Teresa; Nicky Cruz, a former gang member who now travels the world sharing the gospel; and any number of other Christians from all races, nationalities and eras are inspiring testimonies to the way the Word of God can transform lives.

2

THE POWER OF
BIBLE STUDY

It was the fourth day of our camp. We were at a retreat center on the beautiful Hudson River in New York state, spending the week studying the first half of the Gospel of Mark. The idea of spending a whole week doing nothing but studying the Bible, and only half of a Gospel at that, seemed strange to me. It was 1982, my third year with InterVarsity staff, and I was helping to lead the training. I had gone to the camp with trepidation and curiosity.

On this day we were really into it. We had spent about eight hours a day, in three two-and-a-half-hour sessions, digging into Mark in a "manuscript" format, with the text of Mark printed out on sheets that we could mark up with our personal study notes. It was really fun. The time flew by. We were learning a lot about Jesus and falling more and more in love with him, as well as learning a lot about Bible study.

Then it happened. We came to the passage in Mark 6 where

Jesus feeds the five thousand. It was a familiar story, but we saw it in a new light. Digging deep into the text and making connections back to the Old Testament, we saw that Jesus was reenacting Psalm 23, the "good shepherd psalm." He was trying to show his disciples and the crowds that he was the good shepherd who loves his sheep and provides for them. He was also trying to teach his disciples a "shepherd mentality" of serving and caring for people. But they weren't getting it.

That was followed by the story of Jesus walking on the water in a storm, and again confronting his disciples and challenging them with his love, deity and authority. They *still* weren't getting it. Their hearts were actually getting hard to Jesus.

As we were studying this, we were all overwhelmed with the presence of Jesus. He was really among us, calling us to himself in new ways. He was calling us to reopen our hearts to him and give him full control, to repent of our hardness of heart, to be his shepherds and care for others. He assured us of his power and presence. It was the most amazing experience of my life to that point. It was as if Jesus himself came through the words on the page and encountered us. We met him; we experienced him; we heard him speak in his Word.

Fun Night was supposed to start after our session that night. Fun Night is an important part of any camp, a time for students and staff to let off steam and praise God with their talents. It is not unspiritual. But that particular night we called it off. Imagine—a group of college kids and their leaders calling off Fun Night! Instead we spent the evening in prayer, repentance and recommitment to Jesus.

The next day we called off some of the sessions and went to a local park and shared with anyone who was there the amazing things we had learned about and from Jesus—that he is the King, that he is Lord, that he loves us, that he cares for us. I am a big chicken as an evangelist, but I was boldly going up to people and starting conversations about Jesus, and they were listening.

I had grown up in a great church with fine biblical preaching, and had fully opened my heart to Jesus as a freshman in college. I went to seminary, learned Greek and Hebrew, pastored a church and then joined the staff of InterVarsity Christian Fellowship. Yet at age thirty-three, coleading a student Bible study training camp, I experienced Jesus speaking through his living Word in ways I had never known before.

TRANSFORMING BIBLE STUDY

We had dug into the Word. We had engaged all of our mental faculties and exegetical and analytical powers to study deeply and try to understand what the passage said, what it meant, and how it applied to our lives. We observed the facts of the passages, finding repetitions and contrasts and similarities between words and phrases. We found themes and main points. We sought meanings and applications.

But we did something more. We applied our minds to study, *and* we sought Jesus with our hearts. We sought to hear from Jesus in his Word. And he spoke! He spoke to our minds, our hearts and our spirits—to the very core of our being. We experienced Jesus in his living Word, the Bible. We were transformed by him.

CRUCIAL FOR THE CHURCH

Learning to study the Bible in this way is crucial for all people in God's community, the Church. A belief in the truth of the Bible and a desire to obey its precepts is a foundational value of

28

evangelical Christianity. Evangelicals not only hold to the authority and trustworthiness of the Bible, they place great emphasis on the necessity and ability of laypeople to study the Bible on their own and not depend solely on preachers, teachers and other experts. There are many reasons for this.

Christian people need to be able to articulate biblical themes, such as hope, in a way that will be compelling to their nonbelieving or seeking friends. Believers need to embody biblical priorities through their words and their lives to skeptical or cynical friends, family, teachers, professors or coworkers.

The preponderance of attractive and well-funded cults, especially those specifically targeting university students and appealing to the Bible as the basis of their doctrines, makes it imperative for Christian believers to be able to articulate and live out biblical truth. This is important so that their own faith will remain strong and so that they can engage the cults from the standpoint of a personal and practical knowledge of the Bible.

Christian students face special challenges as they relate to the Bible. Researchers William G. Perry and James W. Fowler have shown that students at universities grow and change during their college years. They move away from the faith of their parents and develop a faith system of their own, often one that is different (broader and more pluralistic) from that of their parents. Without a growing experiential relationship with Jesus in his Word, young people are more likely to accept and practice the relativism of the times. But with a knowledge of the Bible and commitment to personal and group Bible study, young people will be able to construct a deep, solid faith system for themselves that will drive them to live out kingdom values for the rest of their lives.

POSTMODERNISM AND POSTMODERNITY

There is another important reason that Christian believers, especially young people, need to be deep in the Scriptures: the cultural paradigm shift from modernism to postmodernism. A number of contemporary scholars, historians and philosophers believe that "we are apparently experiencing a cultural shift that rivals the innovations that marked the birth of modernity out of the decay of the Middle Ages: we are in the midst of a transition from the modern to the postmodern era" (Stanley Grenz, *A Primer on Postmodernism,* p. 6).

Postmodernism is harmful in many respects. The postmodern worldview is built on the "truth" that right and wrong are relative. One sees this relativism in the culture of postmodernity: anything goes. There is no ultimate truth, so everything can be "true" for you. Anyone's opinion is as good as anyone else's. "Historical" dramas on television or in films can change or invent facts for dramatic effect even if they are completely false. Watch any situation comedy on television, from any studio, in any language, and notice the standards of morality presented on the show. In almost all cases, there are hardly any standards at all. "It can't be wrong if it feels so right" is the basic moral code.

But God is still sovereign. All truth is his truth. Humankind, while hopelessly sinful and depraved, still has the spark of the image of God. Thus, like all major human cultural movements, postmodernism isn't all bad. It affirms the historic Christian view of humans as consisting of spirit, mind and body integrated into a whole. Therefore, postmodernism does not accept reason as infallible, as much modernist thought did, and it stresses experience and community. In an ironic way postmodernism affirms the biblical principle that truth is not only propositional, it is personal. The gospel proclaims that truth is embodied in a person, our Lord Jesus Christ, who claimed to be not just the way and the life but the truth. Postmodernism affirms the Christian emphasis on community and on *knowing* God, not only in our minds but also in the very depths of our being and our experience.

Postmodernism started as a literary movement, so its effects are seen in the way many read and write, in both positive and negative ways. In the teaching of postmodernism there is no ultimate truth, words themselves have no intrinsic meaning. Therefore there is no real meaning in a text. A text can mean anything that the reader wants it to mean.

That is why it is so important for Christians to emphasize that the Bible is the Word of the living God himself. If the Bible is his Word, breathed by him in the power of his Spirit through human authors, then the Bible is the main form of communication from God to humankind. Therefore, the words of the Bible do have meaning, because God intended for them to communicate, to mean something.

We need to rigorously use all of the tools of inductive Bible study to discover the meaning of the text so that we may understand what God is saying. We must not read our ideas into the text, but rather discover what ideas the text has for us. That is the basic meaning of *inductive* Bible study: coming to the text to find out what it is saying "from the text out." I used to say that my purpose in Bible study was to "get a grip on the Bible." That is still true, but more important is the sense that I want the Bible to get a grip on me! Bible study has power in a postmodern society because searching the Scriptures, under the power and guidance of the Holy Spirit, shows us what God, the Truth, is saying to us.

Postmodernism's influence on Bible study is not exclusively negative. With its emphasis on experiencing the communication of a text, on community and on narrative, postmodernity helps

Christians read and study the Bible not only for intellectual knowledge, but to get to know God better in an experiential way. The power of Bible study is as a means to encounter the living God in his Word, hearing from him so that we can obey him and grow closer in relationship with him.

This book is founded on two convictions. First, the Bible is God's living Word in which he speaks to our whole being—mind, soul and spirit. Second, Christian laypeople, especially young people, can and should learn to study the Bible for themselves and teach others to do so. When laypeople study God's living Word with depth and power, God's Spirit moves in powerful ways and true revival occurs. During the Reformation in Europe in the sixteenth century, the Wesleyan movement in eighteenth-century England, the Great Awakening in the American colonies in the eighteenth century, the beginning of the parachurch movements in the United States in the 1940s and 1950s, and the small group Bible study movement in Eastern Europe and Latin America in the 1970s, laypeople were encouraged to study the Bible. As a result, world-shaking revival broke out during those times.

I experienced this revival in my own life at that Mark manuscript camp in 1982, and I have seen multitudes of people in countries all over the world experience the same kind of deep renewal and transformation as they took the time to study the Scriptures and meet God there. The power of God's Holy Spirit operates in the study of God's Word as he speaks to us and illuminates the Scriptures.

The following chapters will provide a blueprint to help you learn to study the Bible in a way that not only will help you to discover the truths in the text but also to hear from God in his living Word.

INDIVIDUAL OR GROUP EXERCISES

1. Do a Bible study on Bible study. Study Joshua 1; Psalm 1, 19, or 119; Proverbs 2; Mark 4:1-20; or 2 Timothy 2—3 to see what they say about seeking, searching, meditating on, obeying and studying God's Word.

2. Think about your goal in Bible study. Is it fellowship with other believers? Learning more about the Bible? Learning God's commandments so you can obey them? Is it to meet the living God and hear from him? Is it some combination of these? How does the method of your study reflect the goal that you have for studying the Bible?

3. Think of a Bible study you were in that really affected your life. What were the circumstances of that Bible study? What made it so effective?

4. Read and discuss a good Christian book about postmodernism, such as Stanley Grenz's *A Primer on Postmodernism.* What are the good and bad implications of postmodern thought for your approach to Bible study? Especially discuss why you think the Bible is true and has meaning.

3

ENTERING THE TEXT

In July of 1992 twelve brave students traveled with my family and me to Albania for InterVarsity's first-ever summer mission to that country. Albania had been one of the most repressive countries of the world for fifty years. Dictator Enver Hoxha was so radically communist that he pulled Albania away from the Soviet Union in the 1960s because he thought the Soviet Union wasn't communist enough. Then he pulled his country away from China because he thought even Chairman Mao wasn't communist enough! Hoxha allowed no contact with other countries except Cuba and North Korea, and he ruled with an iron fist. He was also a radical atheist who imposed strict atheistic rules on his people.

In June of 1991, led by a peaceful student revolution, Albania shockingly threw off communism and started on the rocky road to democracy. Through a series of God-ordained circumstances, I had the wonderful privilege of entering Albania in August of 1991. The Lord led me to the right people, I made the right contacts, and we set up a student mission program for the following summer. By July of 1992 we were on our way.

In the orientation before we left, the other leaders and I shared with the students some age-old wisdom for entering another culture successfully: be open, be flexible, be curious, don't be quick to make judgments, observe everything carefully and, most important, ask lots of questions.

One of the first things we noticed as we landed at the airport in the Albanian capital of Tirana was that communist slogans still adorned many of the buildings. In the communist countries of Europe, the ruling governments had put up slogans on billboards and the sides of buildings. In America, roadside billboards say things like "New McRib Sandwich, This Month Only" or "Coke Is IT!" In communist countries these signs said things like "We Strive Daily for Socialism" or "The Communist Party: Our Joy and Hope." We noticed that the Albanian word *lavdi* was repeated often in these slogans—signs said "Lavdi Kommunism," "Lavdi Partii," "Lavdi Hoxha." We asked our Albanian hosts what *lavdi* means. "Glory," they said. "Glory to the Communist Party," "Glory to Socialism," "Glory to Hoxha."

You can imagine the joy we had as we gathered for worship and sang "King of kings and Lord of lords, *lavdi*, hallelujah!" Here we were in what had been the most atheistic country in the world, joining Albanian and American students in singing *glory* to King Jesus! The word that the communists had used to praise their party and their dictator was now being used to praise Jesus. And our experience of joy and praise had been enriched because we noticed the repetition of the word *lavdi* and sought its meaning.

This principle is the key to entering the text of the Bible. Although the Bible is a living Word through which God speaks to people in the modern world, it is also an ancient document written between 2,000 and 3,500 years ago in cultures far different from ours. Entering the text of the Bible to read and study it means entering a strange new culture. The keys to entering a text of the Bible are the same as entering any new culture: be open, be expectant, observe carefully, and ask lots of questions. This chapter contains tips for entering the text of a passage of the Bible successfully, getting to the heart of the passage and hearing what God is saying in it.

BE EXPECTANT

A leper came to Jesus on his knees, begging, "If you choose, you can make me clean" (Mark 1:40). A soldier said to Jesus, "Speak the word, and let my servant be healed" (Luke 7:7). A woman touched his robe, thinking, "If I but touch his clothes, I will be made well" (Mark 5:28). Samuel was instructed by Eli to reply to God, "Speak, LORD, for your servant is listening" (1 Samuel 3:9). The wise teacher instructs his student to "seek [wisdom] like silver, and search for it as for hidden treasures" (Proverbs 2:4). All of these people were *expectant* as they came to God (or to his Word). They expected Jesus to act. They expected God to speak.

The Bible is God's living Word, through which he speaks to you. God's Holy Spirit is waiting to "guide you into all the truth" (John 16:13). As you approach the Bible, be open and expectant. Pray that God would meet you so that you experience him in his Word; that he would speak to you as a friend to a friend; that he would teach you his truth; that he would surprise you with some new insight or discovery; and that he would transform you over time into the image of Jesus. Bible study is the most exciting thing in the world! Come to it with that attitude rather than the attitude of a distracted student with an unwanted homework assignment.

BE HONEST WITH GOD

As you approach a text of the Bible to study it, you can't get away from who you are and what you are experiencing in life. Rather than repress your feelings, share them with God. Often the passage you are studying will speak to your need. Take time to think through what the last few days have been like for you. Share honestly with God what you are feeling. Share your joys and struggles. You will be surprised at how the Bible will speak to your circumstances as you study it expectantly and regularly.

READ THE TEXT CAREFULLY

Every well-written newspaper news article (not feature articles or editorials) should answer the following questions in the first paragraph: What happened? How did it happen? Who was there? When was it? Where was it?

In the same way, it's important to note the "who, what, where, when, how" when studying a biblical text. To really understand a passage in the Gospels, for instance, it is crucial to note to whom Jesus was talking: the Pharisees? his own disciples? the crowds? a woman? children? It is also important to note where the action takes place: in Jerusalem? outside of the nation of Israel in the Gentile lands of Syrophoenicia? on a mountain? on the plain? by the sea? on the sea? among the dark and scary tombs of Gerasene country? When is the action taking place? at the beginning of Jesus' ministry? during his last week? after his resurrection? And of course it is important to note what actually happened and how it happened. It is essential that you make these kinds of observations in order to understand what the passage is about, what it meant for those to whom it was written and what it means now.

This principle applies not just to the Gospels, but to the letters in the New Testament and the laws and ceremonies of the

Old Testament. Realizing that an aged Paul was writing the letter of 2 Timothy to his son in the faith, Timothy, as Paul's life was about to end adds a special poignancy and power to the study of that epistle.

Get the story straight. Find the main points of tension and intrigue in the story, the main parts on which the story hinges. Note surprises, twists and turns in the plot. Who is the hero? Who is the villain? This is a really enjoyable way to read a passage in the Bible.

Here is an important caveat, however, on asking these kinds of "fact" questions: If you are studying a passage on your own, it is important to first find the *who, what, when, where* and *how* of the story, to get the "facts." But if you are leading a group study, *don't* start the study by asking these kinds of questions. Nothing sucks the life out of a group study and insults the intelligence of the participants more than starting the study with a bunch of factual questions that can be addressed by one-word answers in the text.

Instead of asking a lot of factual questions at the beginning, give the group some time at the beginning of each Bible study session to study the text on their own, then come together and share what they have seen. Train them how to observe well, to mark the *who, what, when, where* and *how* in the text. After letting them make their observations in a few minutes of personal study, divide them into groups of two or three and have them share their observations with each other.

FIND THE CONNECTIONS IN THE PASSAGE

Identify the grammatical connections in the passage: words, phrases or ideas that are repeated; those that are similar or different; those that state a cause that leads to an effect; or a general statement that breaks down into specific components.

When people go to see the newest James Bond film, they thrill to the awesome special effects, the new car, the new gadgets, the clever product placement, the evil villain, the plucky damsel and the fearless hero. But the line that audiences wait for in each film is when James introduces himself. "Bond . . . James Bond," he always says, usually while looking suave in a tuxedo and holding his shaken but not stirred martini. The *repetition* of that phrase is the trademark of the James Bond franchise.

In the same way, the *similarity* of the Star Wars movies is one of the things that attracts audiences to that franchise. Each Star Wars movie opens with an explanation of the situation scrolling against the stars as inspiring John Williams music plays in the background. Each movie features the latest special effects. Each includes a fierce battle between Good and Evil. Each moves the ultimate story along to the time when all six will be completed and we will know the full story of Luke and Leia, the rebellion, the Jedi Knights, and how Darth Vader went to the Dark Side. It is these *similarities* that keep us coming back.

Embedded in the plot of the movie *Titanic* were all of the *causes* for the *effect* of the "unsinkable" ship settling to the ocean floor: ignoring the ice warnings, trying to set a speed record, a rudder too small to turn the ship fast enough, leaving the lookouts' binoculars behind in Southampton, and an ocean so calm that there were no waves lapping up against the bottom of the iceberg to make a phosphorescent circle that the lookouts could see. Noticing these causes and their effects as they unfolded added to the enjoyment of the movie. So did observing the central *contrast* between the roguish hero Jack Dawson and the uptight upper-class villain.

Noticing repetition, similarity, contrast, and cause and effect adds much to the enjoyment and understanding of a movie, book, play or TV show. Finding these connections is also a key to understanding and interpreting the biblical text. Seeing such relations as the repetition of the word *immediately* in the first two chapters of the Gospel of Mark or the word *one* in Ephesians 4:4-6; the contrast between wisdom personified as a wise woman and folly personified as a loose woman in Proverbs 1—7; the similarity of the verbs as the leper approaches Jesus in Mark 1:40 (*came, begging, kneeling,* saying, "If you choose, you can make me clean"); and the famous cause and effect in Genesis 12, "the LORD said 'Go' . . . so Abram went" is crucial for understanding those passages. Noting grammatical relationships opens up the meaning of the whole passage to the reader. They are also fun to find! Texts of the Bible are filled with them. Finding connections in the text is a great adventure and will form the basis for interpreting the passage well.

RELIVE THE TEXT

Good Bible study engages one's whole being, not just the intellect. The purpose of Bible study is not just to learn things but to experience the presence and power of Jesus and hear him speak. Analyzing the text by looking for specifics like who, what, when, where and how and by finding grammatical connections can become a purely intellectual exercise if we are not careful. It's important to enter the text emotionally, experientially, engaging the imagination. Narrative literature especially invites this approach, and much of the Bible is narrative literature. Seek to relive the text.

As you study, think of yourself as literally *entering* the text. Put yourself into the passage. If it is a narrative, what do you see, smell, taste and feel in the scene being described? Choose one of the characters and "become" him or her. If the passage comes from the Epistles, Law or Prophets, imagine yourself as one of the original recipients of the words. If it is poetry, let the power of the poem and its images sweep over you.

What would you be feeling and seeing if you were one of the Israelite soldiers going out to battle every day and encountering the nine-foot-tall giant Goliath mocking God with his taunts for forty days, as told in 1 Samuel 17?

What would you be feeling and seeing if you were standing among the crowds on the banks of the Jordan River watching John the Baptist, dressed in camel's hair, preaching repentance, as told in Mark 1? What would the atmosphere be like? Would you go forward, confess your sins publicly and take the risk of getting baptized to prepare yourself for the coming of the mysterious One John predicted was on his way?

What would you hear, see and smell if you were standing by the fishing boats listening to Jesus preach at the beginning of Luke 5?

What would you feel and how would you react if you were a slave in Egypt when Moses came and told you that soon you would be free, but then your Egyptian taskmasters made your slavery worse? Or if you were in the desert and Moses disappeared up the mountain and you thought he would never come back?

What would you feel if you were a member of the church at Thessalonica and got a letter from your beloved friend and pastor Paul that said, "As you know, we dealt with each one of you like a father with his children, urging and encouraging you and pleading that you lead a life worthy of God, who calls you into his own kingdom and glory" (1 Thessalonians 2:11-12)?

Putting yourself into a story, reliving the experience, is a way to observe the text from the inside out. Reliving gets you to the heart of a passage and helps you feel the sweep of emotions the text of the Bible conveys. It helps you to *experience* the story, to discover its points of tension, movement and resolution.

BE CREATIVE

Jim Rayburn, the founder of Young Life youth ministry, got the ministry going in the 1930s based on the simple slogan "It's a sin to bore a kid." I feel the same way about Bible study. Bible study is an encounter with the God of the universe in his living Word. It engages all of one's emotional, intellectual, analytical and spiritual faculties. Studying the Bible satisfies the deepest longing of the intellect and the spirit. It transforms lives. And best of all, it is rollicking good fun! Just as it is a sin to bore a kid in youth ministry, it is a sin to do boring Bible study, to ask the same questions week after week and enter the text in the same way.

God is a creative God. He created the universe, and he created you. No two snowflakes are alike, and no two people are alike. As we enter the text of his Word, the Bible, we too need to be creative. Following are some ideas for creatively entering a text of Scripture, either for individual study or for a group.

Act out the passage. This is the simplest creative entry method for a group studying the Bible together. Everyone stands up and each person chooses a part or character in the passage to play. Choose a narrator to read the narrative, then act out the passage. It is amazing how much fun you can have and how much insight you can gain in doing this.

Often when I lead a group in studying Mark 5:21-43 I have the group act it out. This is the story of a ruler of the synagogue who comes to Jesus and asks him to heal his sick daughter. As Jesus goes with the man to see his daughter, he is interrupted by a woman who has had hemorrhages for twelve years. She touches Jesus' garment in faith and is healed. Jesus turns and asks, "Who touched my clothes?" As the disciples and crowd are wondering about this, the woman sheepishly comes up to Jesus and confesses that it is she. She tells him her whole story. Jesus replies that her faith has made her well. He then goes on to the house of the ruler, whose daughter has died by then. Jesus interacts a bit with the mourners, then puts them outside, takes the parents and three of his disciples inside to see the dead girl and raises her to life.

Acting out this passage gives enormous insight into the depth and layers of meaning in this sequence of stories. After the group acts it out, I ask them to debrief their experience. What were they feeling? What did they notice? What insights did they get? What questions were raised for them? Their insights are invariably deep and profound. The person playing the ruler of the synagogue usually shares how upset and impatient he was with the fact that Jesus would interrupt his journey to his house to interact with this low-class, unclean woman. He is the great ruler of the synagogue, after all, one of the most important men in the town, and this woman is an unclean lowlife. Why is Jesus spending time with her when he should be paying attention to the "important" person? Questions are raised, and answered, about what it *really* means to be unclean, what it means to be healed, what having faith really means and what Jesus' priorities really were.

Acting out the passage and then debriefing adds a depth of insight, application and transformation that can't be attained by just sitting around and talking about the passage.

Sometimes, if the group has been meeting together for a long time and is comfortable with each other and with this method of Bible study, and if time is not short, I have a group put together and act out a skit that will bring out the *meaning* of a passage. For instance, when teaching a weeklong Bible study training camp using 1 Samuel, I divided a large group of students into smaller groups of about seven and had each smaller group develop a creative skit that would bring out the meaning of the David and Goliath story in 1 Samuel 17. I was amazed to see the variety and insight of the skits as the students used sports motifs (complete with cheerleaders, sideline reporters and frenzied crowds), political allusions, clashes of good and evil and re-creations of incidents on their own campuses to bring out the meaning of this story. The creative approach helped them read a familiar text more deeply and carefully and develop helpful questions and insights into the meaning and application of the passage.

Journal entry. Another simple way to enter a text creatively is to write a journal entry for the main character. If David had been keeping a journal, what would he have written in it before and after his battle with Goliath? Or after he spared King Saul's life in 1 Samuel 24, when he could have killed him and immediately assumed the throne? Or after he almost got into a blood-guilt battle with a fool named Nabal but was saved from it by Nabal's wife, Abigail? Or during and after the whole sequence of his sin with Bathsheba?

What would the leper described in Mark 1 have written after he was touched and healed by Jesus, then went out and disobeyed Jesus by telling everyone about him? What feelings of inexplicable joy, freedom and perhaps remorse would he have expressed?

"Produce" a movie or drama. When InterVarsity area director Lindsay Olesberg leads a Bible study on Mark 4:35-41, in

which Jesus calms a storm, she introduces the study of the passage by asking the students to pretend that they are producing a movie of the passage. "How would you arrange the scenes?" she asks. "How would you set up the lighting, the music? What dramatic action would you emphasize?" As the students read the passage as movie producers, it is amazing how carefully they observe the facts of the passage. They see little-noticed details like the fact that Jesus was taken into the boat "just as he was" by the disciples (v. 36); that other boats were with them (v. 36); that *after* Jesus calmed the storm he asked the disciples, "Have you still no faith?" (v. 40).

Other creative entry ideas. InterVarsity staffer Sharon Conley has come up with the following list of other creative entry ideas that you might use in your individual or group study to help you dive into a text and observe it.

- **Reporter:** Write a brief summary as if you were a reporter writing a story on an event or character.

- **Eyewitness account:** Write or share in pairs as if speaking from the perspective of an eyewitness to an event. (Imagine that you are on trial and need to give details.)

- **Role play:** In pairs, "be" one of the characters in the passage and discuss responses to what's going on.

- **Dramatic reading:** Ask several people in the group to participate and read the passage dramatically. (This works really well with passages in which there's a dialogue or in a dramatic or antiphonal psalm such as Psalm 29 or 136.)

- **Testimony:** Ask participants to write brief testimonies of one of the characters in the passage. (For example, what would be the testimony of a man from whom Jesus cast out demons?)

- **Five senses:** Read the passage from the perspective one of the five senses: ask participants to pick a sense (touch, smell, sight, sound, taste), have someone read the passage aloud, and then discuss what each "sense" perceived in the passage.

- **Drawing:** Give each group member a sheet of paper with a few square blank cartoon panels. Have them fill in the blocks with drawings of the scenes from the passage.

- **Magazines:** Bring a few magazines, and ask participants to read the text and clip out of the magazines a picture, phrase or article that depicts their response to the passage.

- **Be the recipient:** If you're reading a letter from Paul, learn all you can about the culture of the people who received the letter, (for example, the people of Colossi or the folks from Rome) and imagine that you are the people receiving the letter.

Our group of students had an amazing time in Albania in 1992. We shared the gospel, learned some Albanian, learned to live in and love a culture that was strange to us, and developed friendships with a diverse group of Albanian students that last to this day. But I think that something we all remember was singing *lavdi,* glory to King Jesus, in a classroom where we could still see the outline of the picture of Lenin that hung there for fifty years.

Why was this experience so powerful? We entered the culture well. We observed. We tried to go beneath the surface. We built lasting relationships. And we asked questions. The experience of entering a new culture changed our lives.

The first step of transforming Bible study is to enter the text well. Be open. Be expectant. Be honest with God. Observe deeply. Put yourself into the passage. Relive the story. Seek, search, knock, ask. Remember the advice of the wise teacher in

Proverbs: "Search for it as for hidden treasures" (Proverbs 2:4). Go deep. Dig for the gold—don't be satisfied finding a few nuggets on the surface. The rewards are great!

INDIVIDUAL OR GROUP EXERCISES

Use one of the ideas in this chapter to enter the text of a passage of the Bible you are studying in a creative way. If you are studying the Bible in a group, have the group use one of these ideas to enter a text together. Debrief with the group afterward, asking what they learned from the experience and what they learned from the text that they might not have seen otherwise. If you are leading or attending a weekly Bible study group, try a number of these ideas. Keep it creative! Remember, "it's a sin to bore a Bible study group."

4

ASKING QUESTIONS
OF THE TEXT

As I sat watching the movie *Titanic,* I was getting annoyed by the constant repetition of one situation. Jack and Rose, the young hero and heroine of the movie, were stuck in the bottom of the sinking ship, in the third-class steerage section. Four times they came to gates that led up the stairs to the higher decks of the ship, but each time the gate was locked shut. Four different times they had to run to another gate through the swirling water, then dramatically push the gate open or dive into the water to find the key. In addition, there was another "locked gate" scene without Jack and Rose, just the poor people in the steerage section being locked in and unable to get to the higher decks. I sat there wondering why the writer of the screenplay of the movie repeated that same basic scene five times. What a waste of film, and of my time.

Then it struck me: the writer of the movie was trying to say something really important about the strict class system of the time. The people in first class were all given life jackets and were carefully escorted to the deck to get into lifeboats. But the people in third class, who were mostly Irish and Swedish immigrants and other "foreigners," were locked in so that they could not get up to the lifeboat area. They were basically condemned to death. The author was dramatically illustrating this deadly inequality and discrimination with the repetition of the locked gate to freedom.

Asking the question, "Why did the screenwriter repeat the locked-gate scenario five times?" helped me get a better understanding of some of the deeper meanings of the movie. In the same way, when studying the Bible it is important to ask good questions about the text.

THE BIBLICAL BASIS FOR ASKING QUESTIONS AND SEEKING ANSWERS

For some, the idea of asking questions of the text of Scripture may seem shocking. "Ask questions of the *Bible?* But the Bible is the Word of God! Isn't it heretical to ask questions of the Bible? Isn't the idea to just read what the Bible says and then obey it?"

Usually when we think of relating to God, hearing the gospel and understanding the Bible, we don't think of questions; we think of authoritative proclamation. God is the creator of the universe, the ultimate authority, and the Bible is his Word. Therefore the Bible speaks with authority. "Thus says the Lord" fills the pages of the Old and New Testaments. God proclaimed his name to Moses (Exodus 34:6). He proclaimed the Ten Commandments (Exodus 20). He spoke to and through the prophets throughout the Old Testament. Jesus proclaimed the gospel (Mark 1:14-15), as did the preachers in Acts (2:14-36; 8:4; 17:23). Paul proclaimed Jesus (Colossians 1:28) and felt that his main calling was to proclaim the gospel (1 Corinthians 1:17). He told Timothy to be persistent in proclaiming the message (2 Timothy 4:2). In modern times, Billy Graham has led thousands, perhaps millions, to Jesus by the public proclamation of the gospel.

Yet the Bible portrays another approach to knowing God that is equally valid and important, although it is less obvious: asking questions and seeking answers. The best way to find out what God really says and to understand what he means in the Bible is to ask and answer questions. This is clear in the Bible itself.

Abraham saw one of the clearest pictures of God's covenant of grace when he asked God the impertinent question "O Lord GOD, how am I to know that I shall possess it?" (Genesis 15:8). Moses' relationship with God went deeper at two crucial points in Exodus when he asked God questions like "What is your name?" (Exodus 3:13), "Show me your ways," and "Show me your glory" (Exodus 33:13, 18). The psalmist, who lived close to God's heart, was full of questions (for example, see Psalms 10:1; 74:1). The whole prophetic book of Habakkuk is an extended dialogue between God and the prophet Habakkuk as Habakkuk asks God a series of questions, then waits in faith and dread for God's reply (1:3, 13; 2:1).

In the New Testament, Peter's great sermon in Acts 2 was launched by a question from the crowd (Acts 2:12). Paul's letter to the Romans is built around a series of questions (see, for example, 3:1-3, 5-9; 4:1; 6:1). The book of 1 Corinthians addresses answers to a series of questions the church has asked Paul (see 5:1; 6:1; 7:1). The first chapter of Hebrews begins and ends with questions and answers (see 1:5, 13).

Even Paul's method of preaching was often a dialogue rather than an authoritarian sermon. In Acts 20 Luke describes Paul's last "sermon" to the people of Troas. The New International Version of the Bible says "Paul spoke to the people" (v. 7), but the New Revised Standard Version says Paul was "holding a discussion" with them. He was interacting with them, listening to their questions, framing questions of his own, listening to responses. This dialogue session went on far into the night (so long that one listener drifted off to sleep and fell out the window). After Paul healed the man who fell, he broke bread with the group, then continued the dialogue/teaching session until daylight (v. 11), just like many college students' late-night dorm discussions. The "dialogue method" of asking and answering questions was a powerful means Paul and others in the early church used to convey truth.

Jesus seemed to love questions and dialogue. He commended his disciples and "those with them" for asking him about the meaning of his parables, even saying that the questioners had found the secret of the kingdom of God (Mark 4:10-11). He often answered a question with a question (Mark 2:18-19, 24-25; John 1:48-50). Jesus summarized his view of questions when he told his disciples specifically to "ask and it will be given to you; seek and you will find; knock and the door will be opened to you. For everyone who asks receives" (Matthew 7:7-8). Jesus could not have been clearer in sharing the priority of asking questions and seeking.

The Bible not only encourages asking questions, it calls us to seek answers. David calls the people of Israel to "seek the LORD and his strength" (1 Chronicles 16:11) and promises Solomon that if he seeks the Lord, he will find the Lord (1 Chronicles 28:9). Psalm 27:8 speaks of the heart seeking God's face. Isaiah 34:16 says, "Seek and read from the book of the LORD." And the importance of seeking answers from God is stated most powerfully by the author of Proverbs:

My child, if you accept my words
and treasure up my commandments within you,
making your ear attentive to wisdom
and inclining your heart to understanding;
if you indeed cry out for insight,
and raise your voice for understanding;
if you seek it like silver,
and search for it as for hidden treasures—
then you will understand the fear of the LORD
and find the knowledge of God. (Proverbs 2:1-5)

Notice that in all of these Bible passages I have cited, the emphasis is not really on seeking specific answers to questions, but on seeking *God*. That illustrates one of the main themes of this book: when we do Bible study we are not just seeking knowledge, we are seeking a Person. We are getting to know God better.

So the Bible, from beginning to end—and Jesus himself—encourage asking and seeking as the way to come to know wisdom and truth. More important, asking and seeking are the way to know God, who is Wisdom and Truth, and to know his Word. No wonder good Bible study puts an emphasis on curiosity, on asking good questions and examining the text carefully in search of answers. It is the way to know God and experience him in his Word.

When you enter a text of Scripture, ask good questions. Asking questions gets you to the heart of a passage, to the main meanings. Whenever you are studying a passage of Scripture, get into the habit of asking, "What questions does the passage raise in my mind? What words, phrases or concepts don't I understand? Does the passage turn in any unexpected ways? What intrigues me in the passage?" Then write these questions down.

CATEGORIES OF GOOD QUESTIONS

Whether you are studying the Bible on your own or leading a Bible study, it is important to learn to develop good questions from the text. It takes work and practice to write good questions. Good questions from the text fit into a number of different categories.

Questions that help you or the group envision the scene. These are the kinds of questions that were discussed in the previous chapter, questions that help you enter the text. Who is there in this text? What are they doing? Where are they? When is it? What is happening? Put yourself into the scene or the story, or put yourself into the congregation receiving a letter from Paul, Peter, John or James. What are you seeing, hearing and feeling? What does it feel like to be walking along the sea with the fishermen, listening to Jesus? What does it sound like and smell like?

Questions of definition, geography or culture. What is a leper? What was a leper's place in the society? What is a Pharisee? Who are the scribes? If Jesus taught "as one having authority, and not as the scribes" in Mark 1:22, how did the scribes teach? Where is Samaria and how was it different from the land of Israel? Where is the land of the Gerasenes? Why did the people of a town wait until sundown on the sabbath day to bring their sick people to be healed by Jesus (Mark 1:32)?

Most of these straightforward questions of culture or definition can be answered directly by consulting a Bible dictionary (such as the *New Bible Dictionary* from InterVarsity Press), an English dictionary or a map. It is important to consult these reference works throughout your study. Note that, while it is important to consult a Bible dictionary throughout your study, I strongly recommend that as you make an initial study of a passage, either for personal study or to lead a group, you *not* immediately look in a commentary for cultural background or ideas of meaning. Commentaries are different from Bible dictionaries. They are the interpretation of the commentator. They are valuable to check after you have done some of your own interpretive work and have discovered what you think is the meaning of the passage. Then you can check your insights against the insights of the commentary writer. (See more on commentaries in appendix six.)

Questions that ask the meaning or significance of connections that you have seen in the text. Chapter three discussed the importance of finding connections in the passage: words, phrases or ideas that repeat, that contrast, that are similar, that go from the general to the specific, that indicate a cause leading to an effect, and so on. But notice that chapter three did not encourage you to ask the "why" question, but simply to observe the facts: who, what, when, where and how. But not why. That is because who, what, when, where and how are *observational* questions. "Why" is an *interpretive* question; it helps you get to the meaning or significance of an observation.

At this point, after observing the facts and connections in a passage, it is important to ask the meaning question. One of the most important skills in Bible study is to learn to look at the connections that you noticed and then ask why, to determine the significance of those connections.

That is what I did in the movie theater when I was getting annoyed by the repetition of the locked-in-the-lower-deck crisis in the movie *Titanic*. I asked, "Why is the screenwriter *repeating* this scene so often? What is the significance of repeating the locked gate?" Asking and answering the question of the meaning of the repetition gave me a deeper insight into the meaning of the movie. That is what the students did in Albania when they saw the word *lavdi* on every billboard and slogan: "What is the significance of that word? Why is it repeated so often?" Understanding that it means "glory" in Albanian helped their cultural understanding, their worship and their evangelism.

In the same way, if you are studying Mark 1 and notice that the word *immediately* is repeated three times in verses 14-42, you should ask why. What is the significance of that repetition? If you notice the cause and effect in Genesis 12, "the LORD said 'Go.' . . . So Abram went," think about the meaning or significance of the cause and effect. Or if you notice the contrast in Acts 6 between the way that the early church handled a crisis in verses 1-8 and the way the world handled the problem of Stephen's preaching in verses 8-14, think about the significance of that juxtaposition and find out what the author is trying to say by contrasting those two events.

By simply asking, "Why is this connection here?" for each of your major connections, such as repetitions, similarities and causes to effect, you will add a new dimension of depth to your Bible study.

Questions that capture the tension or point of intrigue in a text. Much of the Bible consists of great stories. Like most great stories, the ones in the Bible often have a point of tension, intrigue or surprise. Ask questions that get to the main hinge-point of a story, questions that capture the intrigue of the plot. For instance, in the story of Jesus calming the storm in Mark 4:35-41, Jesus asks the disciples, "Why are you so afraid?" *after* he calms the storm. The sea is smooth, the storm is stopped, and they are saved. Their boat is no longer sinking. Yet they are still afraid! Why? What is really going on in that story? What is the story really about? Pondering the tension in a story will help you go much deeper into the meaning of the text.

Questions that link the lives of those studying to the text. The Bible was written not just to give knowledge, but to transform lives. Therefore it is important to enter the text of Scripture with one's own life in mind. Not just at the end, but throughout a study of the passage, either individually or as a group, it is important to keep asking, "How does the story in this passage relate to the story of my life? How does it connect to me and how do I connect to it?"

Questions that tie portions of the discussion together. Whether studying on your own or with a group, after you have asked a lot of questions about the text and sought to answer them it is important to ask summary questions such as the following: How does this all fit together? What is the main point that the author is trying to make here? Why is this story, or this paragraph, here? What is the author trying to teach the original readers and us?

All six types of questions are important for your personal study or for a group study. If you are leading a group, the different types of questions should be used in combination throughout the group discussion. To write good questions, you will need to immerse yourself in the text long enough to see the scene clearly, feel the tension of the text and have your curiosity aroused.

Good Bible study questions have the following characteristics:

- They are open ended, promote discussion, and have multiple answers. They are real questions without totally obvious answers.
- They highlight relationships in the text.
- They use the language of the group and the text.
- They help those who are studying identify with emotions in the text or link their own experience to the text.

- They are short and concise.
- They are sometimes startling or unexpected.
- They contain a variety of type and breadth.

The main fault to avoid as you develop questions for your own study or for a group is asking yes and no questions. Nothing will kill your own study, and especially a Bible study that you are leading, more effectively than a series of yes-and-no questions. If you are leading a study of the story of Jesus and the storm in Mark 4:35-41 and you start out with "Was it evening?" "Was it dark?" "Was it a big storm?" "Was Jesus God?" and so on, you might as well send everyone home to watch re-runs on TV, because that would be a lot more exciting. You will kill your personal study and any study you lead if you don't develop questions that are open ended and promote discussion.

From Moses through the prophets to Jesus and beyond, God seems to love questions. He loves curiosity. He wants people to seek him, to ask, to knock. Asking good questions of a text of the Bible is one of the most powerful ways to get at the meaning of that text. Developing good questions from a passage is the pathway to a deep study of that passage. Practice developing good questions, whether you are studying on your own or preparing to lead a group study. The payoff will be a great Bible study.

INDIVIDUAL OR GROUP EXERCISES

Choose a short passage of the Bible and write down as many questions as you can derive from that one text. Remember, do not use yes-and-no questions. Then take all of your questions and put them in the six categories mentioned in this chapter. If you are in a Bible study group, share all of your questions together and see how many you come up with. Then rejoice, because in developing and sharing questions about a passage you are not only going deeper into the meaning of the text, you are actually starting to create a Bible study on that passage that you can use to lead others into that text!

5

ANSWERING
YOUR QUESTIONS

One of Jesus' statements had always bothered me. In Mark 9:1 he says to his disciples, "Truly I tell you, there are some standing here who will not taste death until they see that the kingdom of God has come with power." In my first, shallow reading of "the kingdom of God has come with power" I assumed Jesus meant his second coming. So it seemed to me that Jesus was saying that his second coming would come before some of the disciples died. But he didn't. That really shook me up. What did he mean when he said that he would come back before some of the disciples died?

I checked some commentaries, but they were not all that helpful. I also listened to a few liberal critical scholars who said that this was clearly a mistake in the Bible. According to these scholars, Jesus, or the "Markan community," really believed that Jesus' second coming would be within the first generation of the church. And he was mistaken. So the solution to this dilemma, according to the critical scholars, was that Jesus was wrong. I must say that was hard to swallow. It really shook my faith.

Then I listened to some hyperspiritual preachers who said that Jesus wasn't really talking to the disciples, he was talking to *us*. What he meant was that he would come back in *our* lifetime—so get ready, because this passage "proves" that Jesus is coming back in our lifetime. Now, Jesus may indeed return in our lifetime—may it be so, *maranatha*—but I could not see that this text supported that idea at all. He was clearly talking to his disciples about his kingdom coming with power in *their* lifetime. So by checking with the critical scholars and the hyperspiritual preachers, all I got was more confused.

Finally, I decided to get on my knees, pray to God for wisdom and check the text again, more carefully this time. I also decided to check the context. I read the story that comes after Mark 9:1. It is the story of the transfiguration in Mark 9:2-13. Shortly after saying "Truly I tell you, there are some standing here who will not taste death until they see that the kingdom of God has come with power," Jesus takes three of his disciples to a high mountain where he is transfigured before them. His clothes become dazzling white, and Moses and Elijah, representing the law and the prophets, appear and talk with Jesus.

Here it was—the answer to my question! In verse 1 Jesus didn't say, "My second coming will happen before you all die," but rather "The kingdom of God will come with power" before they all die. Then, in the next verse, three of them get to see the kingdom of God "come with power" as they see who Jesus really is, transfigured before them as the king, talking to the representatives of the law and prophets of the Old Testament. They *did* see the kingdom of God come with power! Jesus wasn't wrong. The very next verse shows that he fulfilled what he predicted.

In the last chapter you were encouraged to develop a series of questions on a passage you are studying. Once you have generated a series of questions from a passage of the Bible, where do you go to find answers? Most people's first response is "my pastor" or "a commentary." Going to an "expert" for answers, either a living expert in the form of a local pastor or theologian or an expert book such as a commentary, is the last thing you should do. Literally. Do it, but do it last. If you are really trying to study the Bible deeply and carefully and want to discover the truth of the Bible for yourself so that it transforms you, here are some other places to go first to look for answers to questions the text may raise.

THE TEXT ITSELF

It is not just a cliché that the Bible is its own best interpreter. It really is true. The first and best place to find answers to questions that may arise as you read a portion of Scripture is the text itself. Carefully rereading and studying the text you are reading and approaching it from different angles will often give deep insights into many of the questions you have about that text.

For instance, if you are reading the story of Jesus calming the storm in Mark 4:35-41, a question that may leap into your mind as you read the end of the passage might be, "Why would the disciples ask 'Who is this?' after they have seen Jesus calm a storm and in fact have been with him for four chapters of Mark already? Don't they know who he is?" The text itself may contain some clues to the disciples' understanding of Jesus at that point. During the storm Jesus is asleep on a cushion (v. 38), not exactly a Messiah-like action. Even more revealing is the fact that

61

when they woke him up they called him "Teacher" (v. 38). These two bits of evidence from the text demonstrate that the disciples had an incomplete understanding of the fullness of Jesus at that point in their relationship with him.

So we should not be shocked that the disciples were surprised when he got up from slumber and calmed the storm, something no mortal, not even a great teacher, can do. Their question at the end reveals that they are starting to realize that Jesus is more than they thought he was. This insight can be gleaned simply from a careful rereading of the text.

THE CONTEXT

The history of the church is littered with well-meaning and not-so-well-meaning people who got into trouble and created major heresies by taking a verse or passage of the Bible out of the context in which it is embedded. One of the most famous examples of this is the phrase "Let us eat, drink and be merry." Cynics often quote this to Christians and say, "See, the Bible says to eat, drink and be merry, so come on, join us at our drunken party!" Actually, that phrase or its variation appears three times in the Bible. The first time it appears is in Ecclesiastes 8, when it is mentioned in a paragraph about the meaninglessness of life apart from God. The second time is in Isaiah 22:13, in the midst of a section in which God is promising severe judgment on his people for having this frivolous attitude instead of depending on him. The third time, it is said by the "rich fool" in Luke 12:19 just before God says to him, "You fool! This very night your life is being demanded of you." Yes, the Bible does say "eat, drink and be merry," but in each case the context points to the fact that God does not want people to live like that. The context shows that the Bible does not condone this attitude, but condemns it!

Context is especially important in narratives, such as the Gospels and Acts in the New Testament; in the historical books of the Old Testament; and in the letters of the New Testament in which the author makes logical points based on what he has said previously. Because narratives, histories and letters make up most of the Bible, we see how crucially important context is. It is especially important in the Gospels, which are not strict biographies of Jesus but rather true stories about him and his teachings, put together by the books' authors to create certain themes and make certain points.

When studying a Gospel, it is more important to look at the stories or teachings that came before and after the story you are studying than to look at the parallel story in another Gospel. The other Gospel writer may be using that story to make a different, or at least differently shaded, point.

In Mark 4:35-41, for instance, the storm story is introduced in verse 35 with the words "that day." So the question may arise, "What day was it?" Looking back at the context, we see that Jesus had been teaching all day, his first long teaching recorded by Mark. So it was a day when Jesus had been telling parables, relating to people, answering questions and interacting all day. When evening came he got into a boat "just as he was" (v. 36). Knowing the context—the fact that he was teaching and interacting with people all day—reveals some helpful clues about what Mark meant by "just as he was." He was tired! Also, it helps us understand why the disciples would call him "Teacher" when they woke him up in verse 38.

Another helpful example of this in a more controversial passage is Ephesians 5:22-24, where Paul exhorts wives to submit to their husbands as to the Lord. These three verses, taken out of context, could be and in fact have been used by men to abuse their wives in the name of God and make their wives virtual slaves. But read the context. The verse before Ephesians 5:22 says, "Submit *to one another* out of reverence for Christ" (NIV, italics mine), and the section after these verses (vv. 25-33), which is more than twice as long, contains a strong exhortation to husbands to love their wives as Jesus loves the church, sacrificing for her and caring for her in tender love.

Putting the whole teaching together in context, it looks more like Paul is exhorting both husbands and wives to submit to each other in mutual love and care, the wife specializing in respect for her husband and the husband being especially careful to love his wife sacrificially. This does not describe slavery or abuse; it describes true partnership and love. But one sees this only by carefully studying the context.

Looking more deeply at the text itself and the context of a passage you are studying will answer many of the questions that you might raise about the meaning of a passage.

A BIBLE DICTIONARY, ENGLISH DICTIONARY OR MAP

We have already discussed how almost all factual or cultural questions can be answered with a Bible dictionary, English dictionary or map. In the Mark 4 storm story, one can look up *stern* in an English dictionary and see that it was the back of the boat; look at a map of Bible times and see that Jesus and the disciples were on the Sea of Galilee, going east from Capernaum to the non-Jewish region of the Gerasenes (the "Decapolis"); and look up *storms* in a Bible dictionary and see that they often appeared without warning and at night.

Since we did not grow up in the Middle East two thousand years ago and most of us are not conversant with the culture of the times, a Bible dictionary, map and English dictionary are invaluable tools of Bible study. They help us picture the scene and understand the words and places mentioned in the Bible.

THE OLD TESTAMENT

If you are studying a passage in the New Testament, going back to the Old Testament is an important way to answer questions you may have. The Gospels, Acts, the letters of Paul and the other letter writers, the teaching of the book of Hebrews, and even the book of Revelation are all filled with Old Testament references, allusions and imagery. I cannot imagine how anyone could try to understand the New Testament without understanding the Old Testament.

Get a Bible with cross-references that will point you to the Old Testament passage quoted or alluded to in the New Testament passage you are studying, if there is one, and look it up. Remember also that the Bible was not divided into verses and chapters until hundreds of years after it was written. Therefore, don't just read the verse in the Old Testament that the New Testament quotes, but rather, read the whole section.

When Jesus quoted Psalm 22:1 on the cross, "My God, my God, why have you forsaken me?" he probably was referring to the whole psalm, which seems to describe a crucifixion similar to the one Jesus was experiencing. So it is important to read the whole section and not just a verse or phrase if you are going to understand the Old Testament allusion.

In the storm passage in Mark 4, the question could be raised as to why the disciples were in such awe when they saw Jesus calm the storm. Why would calming a storm cause them to wonder whether he was more than a great teacher? There is a powerful parallel passage in Psalm 107:23-32 that describes some sailors experiencing a storm at sea with language and images that Mark seems to echo. The waves lift up high (Psalm 107:25), they mount to the heavens (v. 26), the sailors are terrified and confused (vv. 26-27), they cry out to God (v. 28), and then there is a sudden calm (vv. 29-30) as the storm is stilled.

But in Psalm 107 it is *God* who calms the storm! God actually causes the storm (v. 25), the sailors cry out to him for help (v. 28), he calms the storm (vv. 28-29), and then they praise him (vv. 31-32).

The disciples in the boat with Jesus were Jewish men, which means they would have been trained in the basic knowledge of the Old Testament. As seamen, they certainly would have known the passage about the storm and the sailors in Psalm 107.

Their teacher just calmed the storm. In the psalm, God calms the storm. In both situations there is a sudden calm. No wonder they were in awe! No wonder they asked, "Who then is this, that even the wind and the sea obey him?" "Could our teacher, the guy asleep in the stern, be more than a teacher? Could he be . . . God?" Jesus used the storm and his calming of it to drive his disciples to a deeper understanding of who he is, or at least a deeper questioning of who he might be. One comes to this understanding of the passage by pondering the Old Testament allusion that Mark used as he told the story.

Asking questions of a text of the Bible is the most important action you can take to help get to the meaning of the passage. Once you have raised the questions, check the text itself, the context, a Bible dictionary and the Old Testament for answers. This will drive you deep into the passage and give you rich insights as to its meaning and application.

SUMMARIZING THE MAIN POINTS

Have you ever listened to someone who is rambling along, telling one story after another with no apparent connection between them? Perhaps you finally couldn't stand it any longer, and you broke in and asked, "What is your point?"

In the same way, when you study the Bible, especially after you have asked and answered questions, it is important to sit back and ask yourself what the main point or points of the passage are.

Your summary should tie together the main elements of the passage. It should be a succinct, punchy statement that captures the theme or themes of the passage, as well as its tension and drama. It could be a sentence or a short paragraph.

If you are leading a group study, it is important to summarize the study after leading the group in asking and answering questions. You should have prepared a summary statement beforehand, but throughout the study you also must listen to the way that the Holy Spirit is leading the group into the truths of the passage, so that your final summary ties together both the main teachings and the way that the group has experienced and defined the teachings. Here is a possible summary of the point of the storm passage in Mark 4:35-41:

Jesus is using the storm in the disciples' lives to reveal their understanding of him and drive them to a deeper faith, a deeper understanding of him. He is proving that he can calm storms, but he is also proving that he is more than they expected.

The habit of asking questions, coming up with answers and then summarizing the main point or points helps you go deep in your Bible study. It is a pathway to the main truths of the passage. It also helps you meet Jesus in the text, experience more of him and hear from him as he speaks to you and transforms you through his Word.

INDIVIDUAL OR GROUP EXERCISE

Throughout the last two chapters we have used the story of Jesus calming the storm in Mark 4:35-41 to give examples. By yourself or with your group, put this all together by creating a study of this great passage. First, enter the text and observe everything that you see there. Relive the text. Become one of the disciples in the boat. What are you experiencing, thinking, feeling in each part of the story? Then list some sample questions and answers from the passage, and identify which of the four sources the answers might have come from. Finally, write your own summary statement that encapsulates the main teachings of the text.

After you have created your own study, check the sample study of Mark 4:35-41 that Lindsay Olesberg and I developed (appendix one). But remember, no cheating! Come up with your own study first.

6

APPLYING THE BIBLE

I was facing an enormous challenge. I was the pastor of a church in New Jersey. I loved the people in the church. I loved ministering God's Word to them in private visits, in counseling situations, in weekly Bible studies, and in sermons every Sunday morning. We lived in a comfortable parsonage in a nice neighborhood, just right for our young family with three children under four years old.

Then God did a shocking thing. Through much prayer and soul-searching, a lot of time in the Scriptures, and the wise counsel of others, God called me to leave the traditional pastoral ministry and join the staff of InterVarsity Christian Fellowship, investing my life into the lives of university students.

The work of InterVarsity staff is still a ministry of the Word, still a pastoral ministry, but with some significant differences. There was no church building—the students and I used whatever rooms we could get on the campus to have our meetings. The "congregation," the student group, was not a stable ongoing community. It was a community, but its membership completely turned over every four years as students entered the university and then graduated. Instead of a beautiful wooden pulpit, I preached to the students with my notes on top of a small overturned garbage can that sat on top of a classroom chair. Instead of caring for a nice, stable congregation, my ministry was to encourage and train a diverse group of young believers to form a witnessing community to share the gospel in creative ways and grow together as radical disciples of Jesus in the milieu of the secular university. Then there was the most significant difference of all: I had to raise my own financial support.

As pastor of a church, my salary was adequate for our needs. The church gave us the use of a parsonage and a car, as well as a good benefits package and pension plan. Because InterVarsity is a mission, and I was now a missionary, I had to do what all missionaries do: raise 100 percent of my salary, plus my entire support and benefits package, to the tune of $30,000 a year! I had to find 100 people willing to give $25 a month to my ministry, 50 people willing to give $50 a month, or whatever combination I could find to equal $2,500 a month.

My parents were aghast. Some folks in my congregation were angry. My family was afraid. I felt like little David facing the giant Goliath of fundraising.

Just as I was feeling like David, I actually studied David, preparing the story of David and Goliath for a sermon. As I immersed myself in the familiar story I had heard since Sunday school, I realized that this story, written three thousand years ago, was my story.

While studying the story of David as he faced the giant, I wove my story and my situation into the ancient text. David was young. He wasn't really supposed to fight Goliath—he was supposed to bring provisions for his brothers. I was young, and I certainly had not planned on becoming an InterVarsity staff person. There wasn't even an InterVarsity chapter at the college I had attended. David's older brothers thought he was stupid and vain for wanting to fight Goliath. Some older brothers and sisters in the Lord thought the same of me for leaving the traditional pastorate and joining a parachurch ministry.

When King Saul questioned whether David would be able to defeat Goliath, David remembered how God had been with him in the past as he fought lions and bears. David said, "The LORD, who saved me from the paw of the lion and from the paw of the bear, will save me from the hand of this Philistine" (1 Samuel 17:37). In my despair, as I faced the task of raising my support money, I remembered how the Lord had been faithful in providing abundant income for the church I pastored when I had challenged them to raise their missions giving as a church. If God had been faithful in providing for the church when we trusted him, he would be faithful in providing for me now as I trusted him with my life.

David tried on King Saul's armor, but it didn't fit. He had to be himself and use the resources God had given him. I determined to be myself and use the gifts God had given me, not try to become a slick fundraiser. I tried to honestly share the need with friends, family and colleagues.

Finally, when the giant taunted David, he replied with this memorable line: "You come against me with sword and spear and javelin, but I come against you in the name of the LORD Almighty. . . . All those gathered here will know that it is not by sword or spear that the LORD saves; for the battle is the LORD's and he will give all of you into our hands" (1 Samuel 17:45, 47

NIV). That is exactly how I felt. The battle on the campus was God's. He wanted to bring students to himself. He wanted to establish witnessing communities of students on the secular campus who would share his love, grace and justice. He had called me to join this battle. So the fundraising "battle" was his also. He would provide.

The Lord did "slay my Goliath" of fundraising. He provided all of the support within a few months. Seven years later, when we felt God's call to move to the overseas mission field and serve him among students in Eastern Europe, he provided the 50 percent increase in financial support that we needed to live and minister in Europe. Today he is providing again as we anticipate another move from the United States to the overseas mission field.

Even more important, I learned through that initial fundraising experience how a situation I was facing in the twentieth and twenty-first centuries was the same as a crisis God's people faced three thousand years before, and how the story of God's faithfulness to David was, in a sense, my story. As I wove my story into David's story, God transformed my story and filled me with faith and hope.

Bible study needs to be transforming. It should affect our lives in specific ways. As a wise person said, "The Bible is not given to add to our knowledge, but to change our lives." Paul says the same thing in 2 Timothy 3:16-17 when he says that all Scripture is breathed by God and useful for "teaching, rebuking, correcting and training in righteousness" (NIV) so that God's people may be equipped for every good work. *Rebuking, correcting, training* and *equipping* are action words. That is what studying the Bible should do for us. It needs to transform us into the image of Christ in practical ways.

WEAVE IT IN

How do we apply the Bible to our lives? How do we let the ancient text speak to our situations thousands of years after it was written? The first thing to remember is that the Bible is God's *living* Word. It is an ancient text, but it is a relevant text through which God speaks to us in our present situations. Second, remember the Holy Spirit. It is the job of the Holy Spirit to guide us into all truth (John 16:13). It is the Holy Spirit who illumines the Scriptures and applies them to our lives. The Word is the sword of the Spirit (Ephesians 6:17). The Holy Spirit speaks through the Bible to make it relevant to us, using the Word to cut deeply into us, to penetrate to the very depths of our being (Hebrews 4:12).

So the job of applying the Bible and transforming us through the Word is really the job of the Holy Spirit. But what is our part? The main image that most of us have for applying the Bible is that of a rule book. We open the rule book, read the rule that applies, and obey it. Open and shut. Case closed.

But as I have been studying and teaching the Bible for thirty-five years, immersing myself in it, I have come to a shocking conclusion: the Bible is not a rule book. The Bible does contain rules and commands, but actually it is closer to a love letter than a rule book. The Bible is God's Word, the way he relates to us, the way he reveals himself to us. He didn't send us a disembodied rule book; he sent us himself. He sent us his Word. He wants us to obey him, but doesn't want blind obedience without relationship. He wants our love (Hosea 6:6).

One doesn't really have to know the author of a rule book in order to obey. Committees, boards, meetings and parliaments all over the world use *Robert's Rules of Order,* and very few people know who "Robert" was. They just obey the rules.

But God is different from Robert. He wants to be known (Jeremiah 9:23-24).

The Pharisees of Jesus' time treated the Bible as a rule book. They knew every jot and tittle of the law and tried to obey every last little provision, sometimes to ridiculous extremes. Yet the ones Jesus talked to didn't really seem to know God. The Messiah they were waiting for throughout the generations was standing right in front of them, fulfilling all of the Old Testament prophecies, and they missed him! They obeyed the small, obscure rules and missed things like justice, mercy and faithfulness (Matthew 23:23). They obeyed the letter of the law and missed the spirit of it. They didn't know the author of it. We need a different image for applying the Bible than the rule book analogy.

The picture that I like best for application, although it too is flawed, is the weaver's loom. The weaver's loom is a machine that brings together individual strands of thread. The weaver skillfully blends these separate strands so that they make a beautiful fabric.

This is our job as we seek to process and apply a text of Scripture. We need to bring together the two strands—the story of the text and the story of our lives—into a fabric in which the story of the text challenges and changes our story.

This is the difference between the weaver's loom image and actually weaving our story into the text of the Bible. The two strands of a weaver's loom are equal. The story in the Bible is not equal to our story. But the story in the Bible should transform our story. As we are studying the text, we need to see the text for what it is, for what it says and for what it was meant to say to its original readers. But we should also be reading the text as our story, weaving our story into the text.

The opening story for this chapter illustrates this principle. I was studying the story of David and Goliath. I had applied all of the methods that are talked about in the early chapters of this book: I found the facts of the story. I found many grammatical connections. I got the story straight. I asked good questions of the text, came up with answers, and tried to discern the main meaning of the story in its context.

But as I was doing this, I also read the text in the light of the "story" that I was living at the time. I was facing the "Goliath" of fundraising. What did the story of David and Goliath have to say to my challenge of fundraising? How could I weave my situation of having to raise $30,000 a year into the ancient story of a young man confronting a giant? As I studied, I could see how David's story spoke directly to my story in many ways. That gave me courage, faith and hope. Learning to weave our stories into the stories of texts that we are studying and letting the biblical text speak to our stories are good ways to see what it means to apply the Bible.

If you are studying the story of Jesus walking on the water in Matthew 14:22-33, for instance, you would first notice all the details of the story: the disciples were in the boat alone; a terrible storm arose; Jesus came walking on the water; they thought he was a ghost but he told them it was him; and so on. But as you are noticing these facts, you should also put yourself into the story, relive it. What would it feel like to be on that boat? What would the storm, the waves, the darkness, the splashing of the sea, and the fear feel like? How would you react if you saw a ghostly figure walking toward you on the water?

Then take the next step. As you are seeing yourself in the scene of the boat and the storm, ask yourself what storms you are facing. Are there problems at school, at work, in your family, with relationships, with finances? Weave a storm in your life into the biblical story. Feel the fear and foreboding. But also hear Jesus' words of encouragement: "Take courage! It is I. Don't be afraid." How do those words speak to your "storm"? How do they encourage you?

Then keep going in the story. Peter steps out in faith on the water to meet Jesus. But when he looks away from Jesus and focuses on the wind and the storm, he begins to sink. Jesus reaches out and saves him. Put yourself in Peter's place. In the midst of your storm, how are you exercising faith? Are you looking to Jesus, or to the circumstances around you? How do you sense his hand reaching out to lift you out of the raging waters even though you have not exercised perfect faith?

That is what it means to weave your story into the story of the text. The Bible will be much more alive to you if you can weave your story, your situation, into the text as you are studying it.

You can do this with any narrative in the Bible. Are you facing a big decision or hearing God's radical call on your life? So did Abraham in Genesis 12—21. He made many mistakes, as you will, but he was faithful. Weave your decision into Abraham's story and let God speak to you, challenge you and encourage you. Are you building something or leading something? Check out the story of Nehemiah's rebuilding the wall of Jerusalem. Are you trying to live God's way and be faithful to his Word in a culture or atmosphere that is not godly? Samuel is your man; Ruth is your woman. Read their stories as your story and let them transform and encourage you.

Are you trying to be a faithful disciple of Jesus? Spend time in the Gospels. You can identify with so many of the characters in the Gospels! Sometimes you will feel like the disciples as they show faith in Jesus and do great things for him. Most likely you will often feel like the disciples in their failure to understand or obey. You may feel like the leper, the paralytic or the woman caught in adultery coming to Jesus in your need to receive his forgiveness, compassion and healing. Sometimes you may even feel like the Pharisees, who opposed Jesus because they wanted to stay in the comfort zone of their own traditions and power.

Are you a part of a church or fellowship that needs an infusion of God's Spirit and God's vision and strategy for growth, or are you a "missionary," seeking to share the love of Jesus in a culture that is not your own? Then you are reliving the story of Acts. Are you facing problems in your church or fellowship group, such as sin, misunderstanding, or relational or doctrinal conflicts? Paul's letters and the other epistles in the New Testament speak directly to these issues. Do you want to get your doctrinal "story" straight and understand the foundational beliefs of Christianity, such as salvation by faith? Spend time in Romans and Galatians. Do you want to relive the whole story of history, past, present and future? Study Revelation (carefully!).

As you study any text of Scripture, use the principles you learned in the first five chapters of this book: enter the text, look for and observe the main facts, develop good questions from the text and seek answers, and try to write out the main meaning. But as you are doing that you also need to ask, "How is this my story? Where am I in this text? How does this text speak to my situation? How does it transform my situation? How am I getting to know Jesus better through this text? What does God have to say to me through this part of his Word?"

Following are some additional tips to follow as you seek to apply God's Word to your life.

JUST DO IT

The Bible is not a rule book, but many places in the Bible do contain clear, obvious, relevant commands. The Ten Commandments, for instance, especially as interpreted by Jesus in his Sermon on the Mount (Matthew 5—7), are a good foundation for living in today's world. Put God first; don't worship idols of any kind (money, career, other people's opinions and so on); honor parents and those in authority; keep a day of rest and worship; don't kill or be so angry at others that you want to kill them; don't commit adultery or lust after someone who is not your spouse; don't desire things you can't have.

The second half of most of the letters of Paul also contain clear, practical commands that are as relevant for us today as they were for the believers in Paul's time. All we have to do is obey them. The letter to the Ephesians, for instance, starts with a sweeping history of God's people from before the foundations of the earth as God called us "in Christ" to be his. Then, after three chapters of meaty doctrinal teaching and prayers, Paul starts his practical section: "As a prisoner for the Lord, then, I urge you to live a life worthy of the calling you have received" (4:1 NIV). The rest of those chapters contain practical advice on what it means to walk in the Spirit and live a life "worthy of the calling you have received."

I am convinced that if all Christians in the world just lived out the simple, clear, easy-to-understand commands in the Bible, the world would be a much different, and much better, place. But don't forget, even the commands in the Bible are not there to turn us into mindless, obedient automatons. The purpose of obeying God is to deepen our relationship with him, to get to know him better. God does not command obedience for obedience's sake, but to strengthen our relationship with him (John 14:21).

FOLLOW THAT EXAMPLE

I love biographies. When I was in the fifth grade I cleaned out my school library's entire stock of biographies of baseball players and eagerly read them all so that I would know how to act when I joined the Yankees as their center fielder. Ever since then, whether devouring the biography of Hudson Taylor, Winston Churchill, Malcolm X, John Adams, Phil Rizzuto or Warren Spahn, I have always learned something from each biography I have read. Sometimes it is an example to follow; sometimes it is an example to avoid.

The Bible does contain some commands to obey, but most of the Bible is narrative. Much of it consists of the stories of the great heroes of faith—Moses, Abraham, Deborah, Ruth, Nehemiah, Paul, Lydia, Peter. Their stories are in the Bible not to entertain us but to serve as a model for us; we should emulate their walk with God and their faith. I began this chapter with the example of how I read my story into the story of David and Goliath. One can do the same with the stories of the other heroes who loved God and followed him. That is what Hebrews 11 and 12 are about.

One of the great things about the Bible is that its heroes are real people. They not only have moments of great faith and heroism, they have moments of failure. This emphasis on the humanity and failure of its heroes sets the Bible apart from other religious literature and makes it much more realistic, giving it the "ring of truth."

For this reason it is important to not only follow the good examples of Bible characters but to avoid the negative examples. These stories are in the Bible to show us what *not* to do. There are people in the Bible whose entire lives model what we should avoid—like King Saul, who never quite obeyed God from his heart throughout his whole life (1 Samuel 9—31), or

King Ahab and his wife Jezebel, who were always working against God's prophets and his Word (1 Kings 16—22).

But usually people are more complicated than that. Most of the heroes of the faith also have their failures. David, for instance, whose faith and courage in facing Goliath I emulated in my fundraising battles, also fell into a ruinous spiral of lust, adultery, cover-up, lies, betrayal and murder in 2 Samuel 11 as he dealt with his sin with Bathsheba. Abraham, the great man of faith, showed a lack of faith when he didn't wait for God to provide his son in Genesis 16 and instead took matters into his own hands, with disastrous results. Peter went from being the man who understood Jesus as the Christ in Mark 8 to being the disciple who denied Jesus in Mark 14. These are all examples to avoid.

CLAIM THOSE PROMISES

Sometimes there is a clear promise in the Bible to claim. If you are a Christian, a follower of Jesus, it means that you are basing your life on the central promise in the whole Bible, that God so loved the world (which includes you specifically) that he gave his only son (Jesus), that whoever believes in him will not perish but have eternal life. Becoming a Christian means committing yourself to actively believe, or claim, that promise.

In Matthew 6:33, Jesus summarizes his teaching on material things by saying, "Seek first his kingdom and his righteousness, and all these things will be given to you as well." The "things" Jesus refers to are food, clothing and shelter. This is a clear promise, well within its context, that as you take the hard steps of faith to put God first in your life and trust him in specific areas, he will provide what you need.

BE SPECIFIC

Sometimes when I ask students what their application is from a Bible study, they will say something like "I am going to try to be a better Christian" or "I am going to . . . you know . . . uhhh . . . have more faith." But when I ask them how they are going to be better Christians, or what being a better Christian means for them, or in which specific area of their lives they are going to exercise more faith, I just get a blank stare.

A wise person once said, "If you aim at nothing, you will hit it every time." Making a vague application from a Bible study is like making no application at all. In a sense it is worse, because if you are making vague applications you may think you are growing in Christ even though you are not.

If you are studying a passage of the Bible, either individually or in a group, make sure you don't leave the study until you have made a specific application to your life. It could be an action you are going to start or stop, a new way of thinking, a new attitude, or something you are going to do or say in relation to another person or group. Is there a command to obey, a promise to claim, an example to follow or to avoid? Be specific.

Your application should be measurable. When are you going to do it or not do it? How are you going to make sure you did it? If it is a change in attitude, how is that attitude going to show in your life and in your actions? If it involves a person, who is it? If you are a part of a Bible study group or have a Christian friend, share your application with them so they can pray for you and help hold you accountable.

As you are studying the Bible, seek to weave your story into the story of the text. As you make small specific changes in your life based on what God is saying to you in his Word, over time those will add up to a life that is truly transformed by Jesus as he lives his life through you.

BEWARE OF DANGERS AND PITFALLS

Dangers and pitfalls lurk as we seek to apply a passage of Scripture that we are studying. We read stories in the newspapers of mass murderers who say "God told me to do it" or of people who let their children die without medical help because of a misinterpretation of a text of the Bible. We encounter cults and false "Christian" religions based on obvious misinterpretations of the Bible. How do we know we are interpreting God's Word correctly?

The Bible was written 2,000 to 3,500 years ago in languages and cultures far different from ours. Yet we are told to not just listen to the Word but do what it says (James 1:22). We know that we want the Bible to speak to us. We want to be faithful in obeying God's Word. How do we avoid misinterpreting the Bible as we seek to apply it to our lives and obey its teachings?

Study deeply. I have attended adult Sunday school classes in churches in which the teacher reads the text and then says to the class, "So, what does this mean for us?" The teacher has skipped to the step of applying the text without ever really studying the text to find out what it says or means! This is very dangerous. Shallow reading of the Bible produces shallow Christians and shallow (often dangerous) applications. If you have been interacting with the first five chapters of this book, you are learning an effective way to enter the text of the Bible and discover the main truths of a passage. It is important to weave your story into the text as you go along, asking what God has for you in this text—but make sure you do a good, thorough study of the passage before you make your final application.

Check the context. Always read the passages and stories that come before and after the verse or section you are thinking about applying to your life. What genre is your passage? Is it poetry? Law? Narrative? How does your passage relate to the passage before it and the passage after it?

Many believers treat the Bible like a kind of horoscope, with a "thought for the day" or "verse to obey for the day." They shuffle through the Bible and let their eyes fall on any verse without studying the context. This is extremely dangerous; it is how cults get started. I will never forget encountering some cult members who were convinced that the founder of their group, who happened to have been born in the southern part of the Korean peninsula, was the new Messiah because the Bible said something about a peninsula and something else about "the South."

Check your interpretation and application against the entire teaching of the Bible. A few years ago I read a very serious, very dangerous, very scary paper called something like, "The Biblical Basis for Shooting Abortion Doctors." The author based much of his argument on an obscure, out-of-context story in the Old Testament. He never mentioned the basic teachings of the Bible (especially and explicitly those of Jesus) not to murder other people but to love one's enemies. Years later that same author was arrested for allegedly trying to kill a doctor.

Jesus said to the Pharisees, "Woe to you. . . . You give a tenth of your spices. . . . But you have neglected the more important matters of the law—justice, mercy and faithfulness" (Matthew 23:23 NIV). Many of us do that as we seek to apply the Bible. We pick an obscure little verse to obey, which may be out of context, and neglect the whole teaching of the Bible.

How can you know what "the whole teaching of the Bible" is? Do you have to read the entire Bible and grasp it fully before studying or applying an individual passage? No. One solution is to do an overview of the book of the Bible that your passage is in before you study the passage in detail. The next chapter of this book will help you learn to do overviews of books of the Bible to help you find their overall themes and main teachings.

The main themes of the Bible are not all that complicated and do not take a lifetime to figure out. One of the great proofs for the Bible's divine authority is that although it consists of sixty-six different books written over the course of fifteen hundred years by about forty different authors in three languages and from a variety of time periods and cultures, they all point consistently to just a few overarching themes.

The Bible is about the sovereignty, steadfast love and faithfulness of God; the sinfulness of people; God's seeking love for us in spite of our sin; the eternal worth and dignity of each person made in his image; the deity, virgin birth, substitutionary atonement, glorious resurrection and eventual return of Jesus; salvation by faith in Jesus alone; the equal importance to the body of Christ of each person who believes in Jesus; and the fact that history is relentlessly moving toward God's future kingdom of justice and peace. Jesus summarized the whole law when he said what we should love God with all of our heart, soul, mind and strength, and love our neighbors as ourselves.

As we seek to interpret and apply individual verses or passages of the Bible, our applications must be in concert with these general teachings and truths of the Bible. If you think that an application from a specific passage might be that one can earn entry to heaven by good works, or that one should murder someone who is doing something bad, or that suicide is a viable option for one who has failed at something, test your idea against the main teachings of the Bible outlined above. Salvation is by faith alone, so you can't earn your way to heaven by your good works. Love your enemies—God is in control, so don't go around taking justice into your own hands. You are a person of eternal worth to God, who sent his Son to die for you and give you forgiveness and life. If you fail at something, remember that God loves you anyway. These brief examples illustrate how terribly dangerous it is to overemphasize one or two verses over the entire teaching of the Bible.

Study and apply in community. Most of this chapter has been aimed at the individual Christian who seeks to apply the Bible. But it is also very helpful to apply the Bible to life in the context of a group of believers who are studying the Bible together.

Checking your interpretation and application of a passage of the Bible with a group of believers who are also seeking to understand and be faithful to God's Word will prevent many potential problems, such as incorrect or bizarre "individual interpretations."

As I read church history, I cannot find one example of a heresy or cult that started with an inductive Bible study group, a community of believers gathered around the Scriptures honestly seeking the meaning of a passage and trying to obey the passage with integrity. All the cults I know about started not with a group of people studying the Bible, but with an individual who was a gifted teacher but who went wrong on a crucial doctrine.

On the other hand, some of the great movements of God's Spirit, such as the Pietistic movement in Germany in the seventeenth century, the Wesleyan movement in England in the eighteenth century, and the Basis movement in Poland and Latin America in the twentieth century, were greatly enhanced and empowered by small group Bible studies made up of ordinary laypeople digging into the Word together and being account-able to one another.

One of the most powerful ways to apply the Bible is to do it as a group. Of course it is good for individuals to let the Bible speak to them and transform them, but sometimes it is equally or more powerful for a group to jointly obey a passage of Scripture they are studying.

When I was a college student in the 1960s, campuses were full of racial hatred and misunderstanding. Race-related conflict reached even our sleepy private college in Michigan. I remember one time when a group of us were studying Ephesians 2. We came to the great truth in verse 14 that God is our peace; "in his flesh he has made both groups into one and has broken down the dividing wall, that is, the hostility between us." We were naive young students, but we decided as a group to try to do something toward racial reconciliation on our campus. I don't know whether much good came of our efforts, but I do remember that our group application set me on a lifelong journey of working toward racial reconciliation.

There are Bible study groups in dormitories of secular university campuses who have taken bold action to witness for Jesus, to share love with the students in their dorms, to share Jesus' love in practical ways with the outcasts on their campuses and in their neighborhoods, and who have done other powerful things for Jesus because God spoke to them as a group and challenged them to take action in obeying a passage they were studying.

Check a commentary. The early chapters of this book exhorted you *not* to check commentaries until you have finished your study. But now you have studied the passage, asked and answered some good questions from the text, discovered the main themes of the passage and thought about how to apply them. Having done all this, checking a commentary written by a scholar who believes that the Bible is the Word of God and comments on the text as it is given can enhance your understanding and application. Wouldn't it be great to have John Stott stand next to you and give you his insight on Romans 8 or to have F. F. Bruce tell you about Acts? Well, you can! They have written their interpretations in commentaries. If you are wondering about an interpretation or an application you are about to make from a passage, check and see what an authoritative and reliable commentary has to say about the passage. But don't forget, do that only *after* you have done the work on your own and with your group.

And don't forget that even the best commentary writers are sinful human beings. Their opinions and works are *their* words, not God's. They may be insightful, but they are not the inspired Word of God. Only the Bible is that.

Watch your weaving. In this chapter we used the image of the loom to exhort you to "weave in" your story with the story of the text. To some this may sound like the postmodern idea of "reader response." This theory of reading says that a text means anything that the reader or the "reading community" wants it to mean. In postmodern theory, there is no ultimate truth, and words have no intrinsic meaning, so the author's intent is irrelevant. Thus, in postmodern "reader response" the reader reads his or her story into the story of a text and actually changes the meaning of the text to make the text become the story of the reader.

This is not what I mean by "weaving our story into the story of the text" of the Bible. We don't change the text of the Bible by weaving in our story. We don't change the meaning of the biblical text. Weaving in our story helps us understand the story better and see more clearly how it applies to our situation. We don't stand over the text in judgment. We don't force the Bible to conform to our ideas. Rather, the text of the Bible judges us. The text of the Bible transforms our stories into the story that God wants for us.

How do we merge these two horizons, the horizon of the text and the horizon of our current life and situation? An important way to do this is to put ourselves into the passage and weave our stories into the story of the text so that the story in the text transforms our story and changes us. But as you do this, remember that God is transforming you through the Bible; you are not transforming the Bible.

Let the sword cut deep. God's Word is given to change your life. It is a living Word, the sword of the Spirit (Hebrews 4:12). Let the sword cut deep into your life, thoughts, actions and attitudes. You are not finished with your Bible study until you apply the Word to your life. If you are preparing to lead a study, apply the passage to *your* life before trying to apply it to others' lives (Ezra 7:10). Be specific. Don't read a text of the Bible from the outside, standing apart from it in judgment. Let it become your story. Let God transform you as you apply his Word to your life.

INDIVIDUAL OR GROUP EXERCISES

1. Take the study you did in Mark 4:35-41 from chapter five and pray about some possible applications to your life. Write them down. After you have written a couple of possibilities, check the application possibilities that Lindsay Olesberg and I came up with for this passage in appendix two. Then choose one of yours or one of ours and apply it in a specific way to your life.

2. If you are in a group Bible study, try taking one session of your study and make an application as a group instead of having each person make an individual, personal application from the text. As a group, do something that constitutes specific obedience to the text you are studying. Be creative. Be inventive. Take a risk. Obeying the Bible as a group could transform not only your group but your lives forever.

7

OVERVIEWING
A BOOK OF THE BIBLE

I love baseball. In 1958, when I was nine years old, my dad took me to Yankee Stadium in New York City. The stadium looked imposing and magnificent. Mickey Mantle made a great catch in center field, Jerry Lumpe hit a home run, and the Yanks won. I was hooked. It also helped that when I was growing up my next-door neighbor was a professional baseball player who took a lot of time in the off-season to work with us kids and teach us how to play ball.

In spite of the bizarre decisions and incredibly poor leadership by those in charge of professional baseball over the years, I am still a fan. I go to every game I can. I sometimes organize my traveling and teaching schedules with the Major League Baseball schedule next to my calendar.

Sometimes a generous or well-connected friend, knowing of my love for baseball, will give me seats in the lower box area, close to the field. Those seats are really fun, but I actually prefer to sit in the upper deck at a baseball game, high above the field.

Baseball is a game of strategy and positioning. In fact, there are long stretches of a baseball game in which nothing seems to be happening, to the great consternation of the casual fan who wonders what in the world is going on. ("The pitcher is *thinking*," I say to my casual-fan friends who ask me why the pitcher is just standing on the mound holding the ball.)

The field is huge, with vast expanses of green. So when the ball is hit and goes flying into the outfield, and runners are scurrying around the bases and the fielders are chasing the ball, it may seem like mass chaos—everyone running around aimlessly. Actually, each player has a specific place to be in each circumstance, and the retrieval and return of the ball to the infield is as well choreographed as any intricate ballet. But one can see and appreciate the pattern, the flow and the beauty of the play only from the upper deck, high above the field. From a field-level seat, everything looks confusing and chaotic—the batter running around the bases, the fielders chasing after the ball. But from the upper deck it is not chaos. From the upper deck one discerns the patterns of the game, and it really does look like a beautiful dance.

So it is with any sport played on a large field that involves intricate strategy. American football is like this (although football features two of the worst aspects of American life—bursts of violence interrupted by committee meetings), as is soccer. Both are better viewed from the upper deck than from field level.

This is similar to hiking. If one is going to hike around an area that is unfamiliar, it is always better to go to the highest point first and get "the lay of the land," to see where the paths and the dangers are, so as not to get lost.

So it is with Bible study. If one is going to study a specific passage from a book of the Bible, it is good to ascend to the upper deck first, to get an overview of the book and a sense of its main themes and patterns. Having these themes and patterns in mind helps you keep the specific passage being studied in its proper context, adding richness and depth to the study. Overviewing a book of the Bible and having the main themes in mind also facilitates more accurate interpretation and application of individual texts and prevents bizarre interpretations or applications (see chapter six). Studying an individual passage without an overview of the book is like watching a baseball game from field level—it's fun, but it's easy to get caught up in the action and miss the patterns. Or it's like going on a hike without a map or a sense of the lay of the land. One could really get lost.

This chapter will present a step-by-step method for doing an overview of books of the Bible. We just entered the gate of the ballpark. The sun is shining. The blue sky is dotted with white, puffy clouds. The field is a beautiful green. Let's ascend to the upper deck and watch the game from that vantage point. We'll get a lot more out of it that way!

GET SOME BACKGROUND

Before embarking on an overview of any book of the Bible, it is good to find some background information about the book. Who wrote it? When was it written? To whom was it written? What were the circumstances of the writing?

It is helpful to know, for instance, that most scholars believe Mark was the first gospel written and that it was written to Christian believers, probably of Jewish background, most likely in the capital city of Rome, a place known more for action than for philosophical thought. This background may give some insight as to why Mark uses the word *immediately* so often in his first few chapters and why he doesn't include any of the literary gems, songs, poems or philosophical statements that mark the beginnings of the other gospels. It is similarly helpful to know that the letter of 2 Timothy was written at the end of Paul's life; that 2 Corinthians was an answer to a letter that the church in Corinth wrote to Paul in response to a letter that we now call 1 Corinthians, and that the physician Luke was the author of both the Gospel of Luke and the book of Acts.

Any study Bible has this information, usually in an introduction preceding each book of the Bible. A good Bible dictionary like the *New Bible Dictionary* (IVP) would also have this, as well as a good one-volume commentary like the *New Bible Commentary* (IVP). It's not necessary to spend a lot of time on this, but a perusal of the introductory page in your study Bible or an article in a Bible dictionary will give you a good sense of the background of the book you are overviewing.

DISCOVER SOME IMPRESSIONS OF THE BOOK

If the book is a narrative, it is fun to compare the first chapter with the last chapter and ask yourself what might have happened in between (pretend you don't know). The Gospel of Matthew, for instance, starts with an emphasis on the kingship of Jesus: his genealogy from Abraham to David to Jesus; the visit of the magi, scholars/astronomers/kings from the East who worship him; the fearful and violent reaction of the current Jewish king, Herod, to the birth of Jesus; Satan's offering Jesus all the kingdoms of the world if Jesus would only bow down and worship him; and much more. The book ends with the glorious statement of Jesus in Matthew 28:18 that all authority is now his—all the kingdoms of the earth are now his, without his having bowed to Satan. Throughout the Gospel of Matthew, Jesus chose the path of servanthood rather than rulership and wound up with all authority anyway.

The book of Genesis starts with creation, hits its high point in chapter 12 with the call of Abraham but ends ominously with the covenant family in Egypt, protected from the famine but with danger looming ahead.

Comparing the beginning and end is valuable only if the book is a narrative, with a sense of movement. Comparing the beginning and ending of a letter of Paul or a series of poems like the Psalms will not be helpful. In fact, it could be counterproductive—for example, you could miss the heart of Paul's argument in the middle of an epistle.

With any book that you overview, you should page through the book and jot down some impressions that you have as you go. Glance at titles, at beginnings of chapters and at the first sentences of some of the paragraphs. What impresses you? What stands out to you? What hits you? Jot down three or four impressions of the book.

DETERMINE HOW THE BOOK IS ORGANIZED

One of the reasons I love baseball is that it is the only major sport without a clock. All other major sports, such as football, soccer, basketball and hockey, have a clock that ticks off a certain amount of time within which the game must be played. Not baseball. A baseball game could conceivably go on for eternity! I would like that, but most people at the game would not.

Even though it has no clock, a baseball game is still organized. It has a structure. It is organized around a series of measures of play called innings. After each side makes three outs, an inning is completed. Nine innings constitute a game.

In the same way, every book of the Bible is organized in some way. Genesis seems to be organized around people: Adam and Eve, Noah, Abraham, Isaac, Jacob, and Joseph. Exodus seems to be organized around events: the call of Moses, the plagues, the Passover and exodus from Egypt, the giving of the law, and so on. The Gospel of John seems to be organized around a series of feasts that Jesus attended. Paul's letters are organized around the themes that he discusses. Psalm 119, the longest chapter in the Bible, is organized around the twenty-two letters of the Hebrew alphabet, each paragraph starting with the next letter in order.

After you have paged through the book and written down some impressions, go through the book again a little more carefully and try to figure out its organizing principle. Is it people? Events? Geography? Ideas and themes? Or some other principle? Then try to figure out which chapters might most naturally be grouped together. Make a simple chart, like the example that follows for Genesis, which shows these groups of chapters or "divisions" of the book. Try to have only three or four groups of chapters. Indicate the chapters included in each group. Give each group a short title.

Creation and Fall, Beginnings, Garden, Flood (Noah), Tower	Abraham	Isaac	Jacob	Joseph
1:1 11:26	11:27 23	24 26	27 36	37 50

(John Seiders, 6/94)

You can do this with any book of the Bible. They are all organized in some way.

Note also that a variety of ways may exist to chart the structure of a book of the Bible. Acts, for instance, can be organized according to geography (Jerusalem, chapters 1—7; Judea and Samaria, chapters 8—12; the ends of the earth, chapters 13—28), people (Peter is the main character of chapters 1—12, Paul the main character of chapters 13—28), or theme (the beginnings and organization of the earliest church, chapters 1—7; the gospel crosses ethnic and cultural barriers to produce a worldwide, multiethnic church, chapters 8—28). If a group does overviews of a book and then shares them together, they don't all have to come up with the same chart. There is plenty of room for variety.

FIND THE MAIN THEME

Use the impressions you have written down and your chart of the book's structure to write the main theme of the book. Here are some clues for discovering the main theme: Does the author state it? What does the title of the book mean? Does that give you any help? Watch especially the introduction, the conclusion and any brief summaries here or there in the book. Or just ask yourself: What is this book about? What message is the author trying to get across? Why did the author take the time to write this book?

Try to write out the main theme in a sentence or two. Here are three possibilities for Genesis, each developed by someone who studied Genesis using the method described in this chapter:

1. God creates, judges and begins raising up a faithful family through whom all the families of the earth will be blessed.
2. In spite of growing sin, God keeps his covenant. He takes the initiative to come to people, love and care for them, and

through them work out his plan to build his kingdom and redeem the nation.

3. God creates, judges sin and begins working out his plan to redeem people (John Seiders, Bob Grahmann and Barbara Boyd, *Bible & Life Level II Teachers Manual*, 1997, *Genesis Curriculum*, p. 78).

NOTICE TRUTHS ABOUT GOD

Next, notice truths about God that stand out to you. As you consider the entire book, what are you learning about God? about yourself? Take time to praise him for the way he has revealed himself in the book.

APPLY THE THEMES TO YOUR LIFE

How would you apply a part of the main theme to your life? Is there anything in this book that speaks to your story, to your situation, as an individual or as a group? How will this book transform your life so that you are living out more of God's story? Be practical and specific. What does it mean to you after studying Genesis, for instance, that God comes to you as he did to Abraham in seeking love, and wants you to trust him and obey him? What specific act of obedience is he calling you to as an individual or as a group?

SUMMARY

Here is a simple way to go to the upper deck and survey the whole field, to get an overview of a book of the Bible:

- Look up a few background facts about the book.
- Page through the book and write your impressions.
- Figure out how the book is organized.

- Make a simple chart of how the chapters can be grouped together.

- Write a sentence or two that describes what you think is the main theme of the book.

- Think through how this truth applies to your life and how to live out the story of this book in your own life and the life of your fellowship or church.

If you commit to take a few hours and overview one book of the Bible each month, you will have the whole Bible covered in less than six years. You will have a notebook with the main theme and outline of every book of the Bible, discovered by you! And your life will be forever transformed as you live out the truths of the Bible.

INDIVIDUAL OR GROUP EXERCISES

Use the outline of the overview method on the previous page to do an overview of the book of Acts. After you have created your own study, check the sample overview of Acts in appendix three. But remember, no cheating! Come up with your own study first. Then, if you are in a small group, have everyone share their studies together and come up with a group overview of Acts. Next month, overview another book of the Bible. Remember, if you do an overview of a book of the Bible each month, you will have done the whole Bible in less than six years.

8

DISCOVERING THE "MANUSCRIPT" METHOD

Paul Byer was frustrated with his Bible study. It was the early 1950s, and Paul was an InterVarsity staff member in the Northwest. He had studied architecture at the University of Southern California, then joined InterVarsity staff. An architecture student, Paul had a visual style of learning. When he studied the Bible, he used a pencil to mark up the text. He began using colored pencils to designate themes, key words and other important facts. But something was still wrong. As Paul himself tells it,

> Something bothered me, although I wouldn't have been able to verbalize it at first. It was just that every time I flipped a page the material I had worked on disappeared from sight, and there was no way to relate it visually to the new pages. One morning it hit me; I had to buy two New Testaments and cut the pages out of both (I was working in 2 Corinthians) and then I could put each page face up and work right through the whole text. So I did this, and

discovered that this opened up meaning, as the internal structure and relationship within the text became apparent, and thus Paul's whole letter took on new meaning. (Paul Byer, "The Ross Letter," unpublished paper, p. 1)

Byer cut pages out of his Bible and spread them out before him on the floor, then marked them up. In this way, the main connections, structure and themes of the passage emerged more clearly before his eyes. He shared this with a coworker, and they got so excited about it that they decided to have a conference for students to teach them this new method of Bible study. Legend has it that Byer sent out a letter to the students in advance of the conference and told them to bring "two Bibles and a razor blade," getting himself into a lot of trouble with parents.

Whatever the reason, Byer abandoned the idea of cutting pages out of the Bible and instead had the pages typed up in "manuscript" form. The pages included only the text of the Bible, with no verse numbers, chapter divisions, chapter headings or paragraph divisions. The text was printed on only one side of unbound paper. In this way it was possible to always keep several sequential pages face up on the table so that the study of any particular section of the text could always be done in visual contact with its context. The text was double-spaced, and a lot of white space was left on each page of text for markings, notes, questions and comments.

Byer and his coworker gathered the students in a conference center in Bellington, Washington, and they studied Colossians for five days straight. Byer commented that "it proved to be a significant time for those of us involved, and we continued this format once or twice a year with other students."

Thus the method of *manuscript study* was born. Under Byer's leadership, the method spread through California InterVarsity and then through InterVarsity/USA. Eventually it spread all over the world through missionaries, pastors and laypeople trained by Byer. They then trained other people to train others, and now Paul Byer's manuscript study is used throughout the world, in countries east and west, north and south, rich and poor, in public and in secret. This one faithful man, fiddling with his colored pencils and his two cut-apart Bibles on his floor, seeking to hear from God in his Word, affected the world.

In most Christian scholarly circles the word *manuscript* refers to a text of Scripture or portion of a text that is an early copy, or copy of a copy, of an original writing of the Bible. These early manuscripts are in the original biblical languages of Greek, Hebrew or Aramaic and are very ancient and valuable. A whole science called *textual criticism* has developed around the study of these early manuscripts. Scholars attempt to compare the earliest manuscripts of the Bible to arrive at the most accurate text in the original language.

But in this book, "manuscript study" refers to a method of Bible study in which the text is printed out on consecutive unbound pages with no verse numbers, chapter divisions, chapter headings or paragraphs, with a lot of white space for writing notes and comments, and then insights are shared in a group context.

THE BASIC METHOD

The basic way to do manuscript study of a text of the Bible is to have the manuscript of the passage and its context spread out before you. The text should be double-spaced, printed on only one side of unbound paper, with just text on each page—no verse numbers, paragraph breaks, chapter divisions, chapter headings or other helps, and with lots of white space. It is helpful to be at a table on which you can spread out your pages of text, your colored pens, and maybe an English dictionary and Bible dictionary.

Where do you get portions of the Bible in manuscript form? You can download texts from a website that allows you to do that, such as <www.gospelcom.net>. Then take out the verses, paragraph indentations, chapter breaks and so on so that you have just the text on your page. Print it off with a lot of white space. Or you can type the text out on your computer. Write to InterVarsity's National Service Center at P.O. Box 7895, Madison, WI, 53707-7895 for other ideas on ways to get books or passages of the Bible in manuscript form.

STUDY THE TEXT ON YOUR OWN

Pray that God would speak to you in his living Word. Approach the text as if you were reading it for the first time, even if it is a familiar passage. As Paul Byer put it, "The most valuable person is not the one who thinks he or she has all the answers, but the one who, having come to the text for the first time, or observing it as though it were the first time, has a dozen questions come out of the text and flood into his or her mind" (Paul Byer and Eric Miller, "Suggestions on Using a Manuscript Format of a Biblical Text," unpublished paper, p. 1).

Then grab a pen, a pencil and some colored markers and begin to mark up the text. Byer wrote,

Mark it up with underlining, circles, connecting lines, '?'s', '1's', '1,2,3's,' etc. We can write questions and comments in the margins or between the lines. Pens or pencils are actively used as the text is read. Many use colors for added visual emphasis as they follow repeated words, phrases, or themes with various colors. . . . The purpose is to observe and actively work on the text, to accent what seems to be significant, and to become involved in a graphic way with it. (Ibid.)

SHARE YOUR DISCOVERIES AND QUESTIONS WITH YOUR GROUP

Manuscript study is by its very nature communal. The basic picture of a manuscript study is a group of people sitting together around a table, studying the text for a while individually, and then sharing their discoveries together.

After a time of individual study, share your discoveries, your observations, and your questions with the others at the table in a free-flowing discussion. No one person should dominate this discussion. Rather, the group itself becomes a community of interpretation around the text in which each person contributes something as the group grapples with the meaning and application of the text, depending on the gifts and insights of each person and relying on the Holy Spirit to lead them into truth. Paul Byer and Eric Miller describe ideal communal manuscript study like this:

Each person studies the text for a time on his/her own. . . . Then when the personal study time is up and discussion begins (they share their questions with each other). This means that questions are asked which are authentic, not ones to which we already have answers. So others are invited into a true search for understanding. In such exchanges, where each person questions and answers with integrity, there is considerable opportunity to learn from each other. The diversity of observation, tested against the common text, allows the meaning best supported by textual data to become apparent. Such teamwork keeps the authority of the text primary. All other ideas are submitted to its data. (Ibid.)

COME TOGETHER AND SHARE IN THE LARGER GROUP

Ideally, a manuscript study session consists of at least ten people. These form a few smaller groups around tables for the initial personal time of studying the passage, then sharing observations, questions, and answers together, grappling with the main themes.

After the time of sharing around the tables in the smaller groups, the leader gathers everyone together in the larger group. The leader starts with the beginning of the passage under study and works through it, gathering comments and questions about the text from everyone. Through dialogue and interaction with the group, the leader helps the group find the main meanings and applications of the passage. All comments and questions need to be accepted and dealt with on the basis of the data in the text. The leader's main responses should not be "That's right," or "That's wrong." Rather the leader should constantly be asking, "Where did you see that in the text?" and thereby constantly drive the group back to the text. The text is the real authority in the group, not the leader. Using this interactive dialogue technique, the leader helps the group come to consensus on the main points and meanings in the text and leads the group to process and apply the text to their lives as individuals and as a group.

Paul Byer described leading a manuscript study large group session in this way:

I was in charge. But, at the same time I was not the authority to determine what the text was saying. The authority was in the text itself, and we all worked together to determine its meaning. . . . Each person contributed to what they thought the text was or was not saying, but their comment had to be supported by the data in the text. (Ibid., p. 2)

Sometimes people think that leading a manuscript study is easy. There is no preparation; one just goes with the flow and lets the group do the work. Nothing could be more wrong, or more dangerous. Leading a manuscript study takes twice the work of preparing an ordinary "go down a prepared list of pre-fabricated questions" Bible study. One has to prepare twice as hard to anticipate all of the questions that the group may raise, as well as all of their responses. One has to know the text really well to know whether participants' statements are supported by it. During the study, the leader has to keep one eye on the discussion to make sure that the group is really getting at the main points of the text, one eye on the group dynamics to make sure everyone is contributing and no one person is dominating, and one spiritual eye on the Holy Spirit to see where he taking the group as he leads them into all truth. That is a lot of eyes! And a lot of spiritual and mental preparation.

Yet it does not take a trained professional minister, priest or professor to lead a good manuscript study. In fact, professional Christian leaders can be at a disadvantage in leading a dialogue-type study because they are often trained to overcontrol and pontificate when it comes to Bible study.

Rather, the best candidate to lead a great manuscript Bible study is a humble believer who is willing to put in the preparation time for study and prayer, who is willing to facilitate a group and watch over the group dynamics, and who is willing to let the Holy Spirit lead the group into truth.

THE ADVANTAGES OF MANUSCRIPT STUDY

1. It's fresh. Looking at a text of the Bible without verse numbers, chapters, paragraph breaks and so on helps one see the text in a fresh way. It helps the students get preconceptions or memories of past sermons out of their minds and see the text in a new and exciting way.

2. It helps you see themes. Other than a few chapters of the book of Proverbs, the Bible wasn't written as verses. Mark didn't get up one day and say, "Today I will write Mark 3:14. That will be an awesome verse." Paul didn't write Romans one verse a month (although some preachers spend a month on one verse of Romans). No, the books of the Bible were written as wholes, as documents. Paul's epistles are letters. One doesn't compose a letter one sentence a day. A letter contains themes that the author wants to get across. The Gospels are whole documents, witness documents to the glory, humility, power and presence of Jesus. Verse numbers were not even added until hundreds of years after the Bible was written. So when studying a manuscript of a passage, with the passage and its context laid out on the table in front of you, it is easier to see the main themes of the passage, the main points the author wanted to say.

3. It's yours. You are free to write on the manuscript, to make marks, to draw lines of connection, to use different colors to illustrate different themes (there is no prescribed color scheme that one must use—invent your own), to write questions and insights.

4. It's discovery. The emphasis is on learning through discovery rather than being told by an expert. One learns more when one discovers something for oneself.

5. It's communal. The truth is discovered by group interaction with a stress on relationships, sharing and listening to each other.

6. It's a level playing field. The authority in the study is not the leader, but the text. There is a level playing field for all participants. No one is ahead of the others. No one is the "expert." Anyone who can read can do manuscript study. In fact, sometimes nonbelievers who are really seekers do better at manuscript study than veteran believers because they come to the text without preconceptions or traditional interpretations that can obscure the real meaning of a text.

7. It guards against heresy and false teaching. Often people worry that the opposite is the case. People fear that letting loose a group of believers on a text will lead to all kinds of strange and heretical interpretations. What is needed, they say, is an authoritative teacher to tell people the truth. Yet throughout history, heresies and cults have tended to start with authoritative teachers who go wrong rather than inductive Bible study groups who honestly search the text. Paul Byer felt that studying the Bible in this way provided three checks against interpretive error: first, the Biblical text was studied within its context, usually through the study of a whole book of the Bible; second, the group interaction was very important and formed an interpretive community in which students checked each other with their contributions; and third, informed scholarship was consulted during the study in the form of Bible dictionaries and concordances. Byer

saw Bible dictionaries, concordances and commentaries as simply a widening of the interpretive community (ibid., p. 6).

8. It's fun!

Try it. Gather a group of believers or seekers willing to put in some time studying the Bible and willing to let the text be the authority and the Holy Spirit be the teacher. Download texts from a website and take out the verses, paragraph indentations, chapter breaks and other formatting, or just type the text out on your computer. Give everyone a text to put in front of them, then dig in! Seek Jesus in his Word. Prepare well to facilitate the group. Follow the steps in this chapter. You'll learn a lot about the Bible. You'll draw closer together as a group. Most important, you'll hear from Jesus in his Word.

INDIVIDUAL OR GROUP EXERCISES

The following page is a "blank" manuscript of the beginning of the Gospel of Mark. Get some colored pencils, pray, and follow the instructions in this chapter to mark up your page and develop a manuscript study. Share your discoveries together in a group.

A "filled-in" version of this page is in appendix four. But don't look at it until after you have done your own study. Also, remember that there is no prescribed way to mark up the text. Anything that helps you observe the text, see the main themes and apply them to your life is OK. Develop your own system for marking up the text.

The beginning of the gospel about Jesus Christ, the Son of God. It is written in Isaiah the prophet: "I will send my messenger ahead of you, who will prepare your way"—"a voice of one calling in the desert, 'Prepare the way for the Lord, make straight paths for him.'" And so John came, baptizing in the desert region and preaching a baptism of repentance for the forgiveness of sins. The whole Judean countryside and all the people of Jerusalem went out to him. Confessing their sins, they were baptized by him in the Jordan River. John wore clothing made of camel's hair, with a leather belt around his waist, and he ate locusts and wild honey. And this was his message: "After me will come one more powerful than I, the thongs of whose sandals I am not worthy to stoop down and untie. I baptize you with water, but he will baptize you with the Holy Spirit." At that time Jesus came from Nazareth in Galilee and was baptized by John in the Jordan. As Jesus was coming up out of the water, he saw heaven being torn open and the Spirit descending on him like a dove. And a voice came from heaven: "You are my Son, whom I love; with you I am well pleased." At once the Spirit sent him out into the desert, and he was in the desert forty days, being tempted by   Satan. He was with the wild animals, and angels attended him. After John was put in prison, Jesus went into Galilee, proclaiming the good news of God. "The time has come," he said. "The kingdom of God is near. Repent and believe the good news!" (Mark 1:1-15)

9

PUTTING IT ALL TOGETHER
FOR PERSONAL STUDY

Imagine that your pastor didn't show up to preach one Sunday morning, and instead the person who ascended to the pulpit was . . . *the apostle Paul!* Yes, imagine that Paul showed up at your church and preached one of his greatest sermons ever. What a thrill that would be! The congregation would be in awe.

That is exactly what happened in the town of Berea in Acts 17. Paul had been preaching in Thessalonica. But when a riot ensued, Paul and Silas had to sneak out under cover of darkness and flee to Berea. When they got there, Paul went to the synagogue and preached. Verse 11 says, "Now the Bereans were of more noble character than the Thessalonians, for they received the message with great eagerness and *examined the Scriptures every day to see if what Paul said was true*" (NIV, italics mine).

The apostle Paul preached and the people received the word, but then they said, "Hold on, Paul. Your message sounded great, but you have to give us a week to study this for ourselves to make sure that what you are saying is true!" This first generation of Jewish people who came to Jesus gave a high priority to studying the Bible for themselves, not just relying on the word of the preacher.

It is absolutely crucial to the present and future health of the church for laypeople to be able to study the Bible well, find the main point of a passage and hear from Jesus in his Word. How else is the church going to grow deep and strong, be able to fend off cults, function in this relativistic postmodern society, be healthy enough to send and support missionaries, and be powerful enough in the Spirit to affect society with the gospel and the priorities of Jesus' kingdom?

In this chapter I will summarize what we have learned so far and present a way that an individual can delve deep into the Bible, find the main points of a passage, hear from and experience Jesus in his Word and be transformed by him. For the rest of this chapter, imagine that I am talking to you directly. Sit down and grab your Bible, some notepaper or perhaps a manuscript of the passage you are studying (see chapter eight), and a cup of tea.

First, some preliminary tips:

1. Study your way through the books of the Bible. Don't just study random texts. Most of the books of the Bible were written as units—letters from Paul, Gospels that paint a picture of Jesus, historical records such as 1 and 2 Samuel in the Old Testament or Acts in the New Testament. Just dipping into a passage in the middle of a book of the Bible can be confusing and frustrating, and failure to account for context may lead to all kinds of misguided interpretations.

2. Do a simple overview of the book in which your passage is

found before you start studying the passage. Chapter seven of this book tells you how to do that. By doing an overview of the book first, you will have a deeper sense of the main themes of the book and the context in which your passage sits.

3. Use a more literal translation of the Bible, such as the New Revised Standard Version, the New International Version or the New American Standard Bible. Don't use a paraphrase of the Bible when you are doing serious Bible study.

4. Get a Bible you can mark up. Better yet, get a manuscript of the passage (see chapter eight).

5. Even though you are studying through books of the Bible, choose *short* passages to study each session. Don't try to dig into a long chapter of Isaiah in one hour and learn everything. Start with a Gospel and study half a chapter at a time.

You have chosen your passage. You have done a simple overview of the book in which the passage is found. You have your Bible or manuscript in front of you. Your tea is hot. Let's dig in!

BE EXPECTANT

God wants to communicate with his people. In Genesis 3 he found Adam and Eve hiding and spoke to them his words of judgment and hope, even though they had sinned. God wants to meet with you! He sent Jesus to be the mediator between God and humankind. He sent his Spirit to bring the presence of Jesus to us and to illuminate the Scriptures. So be expectant as you approach the Bible. Pray that God would *meet you* so that you experience him in his Word, *speak to you* as a friend to a friend, *teach you* his truth, *surprise you* with some new insight or discovery and *transform you* over time into the image of Jesus.

GET HONEST WITH GOD

When Jesus walked with the two disciples on the road to Emmaus, first he asked them to tell their story. Only then did he tell them *his* story, using the Old Testament (Luke 24:13-35). In the same way, as you approach the Bible to study it, first share your "story" with God in prayer. Take time to think through what the last few days have been like for you. Share honestly with God what you are feeling as you approach your time with him. Share your struggles and joys. Ask him to speak, over time, to issues in your life. Ask him to speak to you from the passage you are about to study. Ask him to open your heart and mind to understand his Word. Then be ready to listen to him!

ENTER THE TEXT

The Bible may seem like a familiar book, but it was written at a time and place far different from ours. You have to enter the text the same way you would enter a new city or a new country. Look around. Notice things. Ask questions. Be curious. Have fun.

1. Read the passage carefully and write down or circle specifics that you see, such as *who* is there, *what* is happening, *when* it is, *where* it is and *how* it is happening.

2. Circle or write down words, phrases or ideas that connect by *repeating, contrasting, being similar,* going from the *general to the particular,* or stating a *cause that leads to an effect.*

3. Put yourself into the passage. If it is a narrative, put yourself into the story. What do you see, smell, hear, taste and feel? Choose one of the characters and identify with him or her. Put yourself in the character's place. Relive the story. If your passage is a letter or law section, feel what it might have felt

113

like to get the letter or hear the law. If it is poetry, let the power of the poem and its images sweep over you. Are there ways that this passage is your story? Is there anything here you can identify with?

4. What *questions* does the passage raise in your mind? What words, phrases or concepts don't you understand? Does the passage turn in any unexpected ways? What intrigues you? Write these questions down.

MEDITATE

Bible study is not all cognitive observation and analysis. Remember, the purpose of your study is to experience Jesus, to hear from him. So now that you have done some study, step back and read the passage a few times again. Read it as if Jesus were standing right there with you. (He is!) Ponder again the points that stand out to you. What does the passage say or point to about God? Ask him what he has for you personally in the passage. What area of your life is God speaking to?

TAKE A SECOND LOOK AT THE PASSAGE

You might want to do this the second day. Read through the passage again.

Develop paragraphs. See whether the passage can be divided into thought units or paragraphs. Which sentences do you think add up to a thought unit? Mark them together as a paragraph. (This is why it is good to have a manuscript of the passage. Your Bible may already have paragraphs, but it is better if you create them yourself and discover where the thought units divide.) Then write a brief title for each paragraph.

Try to answer your questions. This part is the most fun. Remember those questions you wrote yesterday as you studied the passage? Now it is time to answer them. Don't call your pastor. Don't run to a commentary. Do the interpretive work yourself. Look hard in the passage for insights into your questions. Look also at the context of the passage. Are there clues in the passages before and after your passage that may help answer your question, anything that connects with or contrasts with a word, phrase or idea in your passage?

If you are studying a gospel or another passage from the New Testament, is there any passage from the Old Testament that might relate to your passage and shed light on your questions? You may want to check an English dictionary, Bible dictionary or map to help you define words or geographic references in your text. Stay away from commentaries until you come up with your own interpretation. If you are studying with a group, watch to see the wonderful way the Spirit works through the group's sharing to bring insight into the passage.

One of the best ways to move toward answers to your questions is to look for connections among the paragraphs. Is there a word, phrase or idea that repeats? Is there a contrast? Do you see a cause in one paragraph and the effect in another, or a string of similar words, phrases or ideas that run through a few paragraphs? Draw lines between the connected words or phrases to mark them. What do you think is significant about these connections? What light do they shed on possible answers to your questions?

SUMMARIZE

Look at your connections, your questions, your points of significance and the context. Step back and ask yourself: *What are the main points of this passage? What is the author trying to say?* Why is this passage or story here? Try to write this in an integrative sentence or short paragraph.

WEAVE IT IN

Like a master weaver, weave your story, your life, into the story in the text, and weave the truths of the text into your life. Relive the story in the text. How is it your story? As you ponder your study, do you sense that God is speaking to any part of your life? Is there a promise to trust, a command to obey, or an example to follow or avoid? Is there a deeper insight into God or your experience with God? What specific action are you going to take in response to what God is saying to you?

WORSHIP HIM

Take the time to worship God and respond to his love for you. Thank him for speaking to you in his living Word.

THE JOY OF COMMUNITY

Finding observations, developing questions, and seeking answers works well for individual study. You can get a lot out of a passage by studying it in the way described here. Studying it in this way will also help you as you prepare to lead a Bible study, teach a Sunday school class, or give a talk.

After you have studied the passage by yourself, share it with trusted fellow believers in a Christian community to get their correction, affirmation and insights. Include at least one fellow believer with whom you share Bible study on a regular basis. Check an evangelical commentary to see how your interpretation matches the interpretation of the commentator.

The next time the apostle Paul, Chuck Swindoll or Billy Graham shows up at your church, you can say, "That was a great message, but hold on! We have to study this passage for a week individually and in our small group Bible studies to see if what you are saying is really true." I am convinced that if every church had individuals and small groups who studied the Bible seriously, seek Jesus in his Word, and then apply and obey what he says, the church, and the world, would truly be transformed.

INDIVIDUAL OR GROUP EXERCISES

Choose a brief passage from the Bible and follow the step-by-step instructions in this chapter to do a complete inductive study of the passage. Don't forget to apply it to your life in a specific way. Share your study with a friend.

10

PUTTING IT ALL TOGETHER FOR GROUP STUDY

We are going to call our group study a "communal discovery Bible study" because the community—the group—discovers the truth of a Bible passage together through asking and answering good questions and seeking Jesus together in his Word. The leader assists the group in digging into the passage rather than the leader alone sharing insights and answering the group's questions.

BASIC OUTLINE

Each communal discovery Bible study starts with a few minutes of personal time for each member of the group to read and mark their texts. The group then spends the rest of the hour sharing what they see in the text, raising questions generated by the text, and grappling with those questions as a group as they seek answers from the text. The leader helps summarize the main points or flow of the passage. Finally, the group discusses how the passage relates to them and how they could apply it.

The leader's role is to facilitate the discussion and the discovery process and to help keep the group focused on seeking to meet Jesus in his Word and experience his presence and power.

OUTLINE OF A ONE-HOUR COMMUNAL DISCOVERY BIBLE STUDY

Introduction (1 minute)

Take a minute (a little longer the first day) to introduce the inductive method and the passage.

Prayer and Individual Study (5 minutes)

Give your group about five minutes to study the passage individually. You could suggest a creative way to have your group look at the text—choose one from the many suggestions in chapter three of this book. Or you can teach the three basic ways to study a text:

1. Look for the specifics, such as who, what, when, where and how.

2. Look for connections within the text, such as repetitions and contrasts.

3. Enter the text experientially by becoming one of the characters in the story.

Share Observations and Questions Together (15 minutes)

• This time should be lively. You could have participants share their responses to the creative "enter the text" exercise and let that generate the observations and questions. Or you could ask, "What do you see here, and what questions do you have?" The emphasis is on the group sharing what they have seen in the text.

- Note their questions, but tell the group to hold off on answering them.

Answer Questions Together (24 minutes)

- Divide your group into smaller groups and let each smaller group pick a question or two and work on it together for a few minutes.

- Remind them of the four places to look as they seek answers to the questions: the text itself; the context; the Old Testament, if you are in a New Testament passage; and a Bible dictionary, English dictionary and map to find the answers to factual or cultural questions. (Do not use a commentary during the study.)

- Call everyone together and walk through the passage again from beginning to end, then have the group answer the questions together. Blend each smaller group's findings into a group consensus of answers as you go through the questions in the order of the way they appear in the passage.

- Encourage the group to base their answers on evidence from the text itself and the context.

- The twenty-four minutes spent answering the questions together that the group generated are the heart of your study.

- If you have helped the group observe well, the group becomes self-correcting. Keep them in the text; help them develop good questions and answer them from the passage, its context, and the Old Testament background; and work toward a group consensus in answering the key questions.

Summarize (5 minutes)

After walking through the passage and answering the questions as a group, a few main themes should emerge. Summarize these themes with a few sentences or a paragraph.

Process and Apply (10 minutes)

- Help the group to process and apply the passage. Have about four possible application questions in mind before the study, but use only two of them. Throughout the study, be attentive to where the Holy Spirit is leading the group. What themes are they really seeing in the text? Ask the application questions based on what the group has discovered as the main themes.

- Make sure you leave about ten minutes for this process. This is the time when the Holy Spirit will solidify what he has been speaking to the group about in the study. He will transform the individuals and the group by his Word as they make specific applications and then do them.

Remember that you are the facilitator of the group's learning. Trust Jesus, the text and the Holy Spirit to be the authorities. Have the main teachings and a main truth statement in mind, but trust the Holy Spirit working through the group to come up with a good interpretation and application of the passage. Phrase the main teachings in the language of the group.

Leading the Study

- Study the passage for yourself first. The previous chapter describes a way that you can study a passage on your own. Use this method to prepare the study yourself. You could prepare your study during your daily devotions or quiet times, or set aside a special time to prepare. Preparing each study should take you about an hour and a half, or two forty-five-minute quiet times.

- As you study each passage, make sure that you make a personal application from the passage. What is Jesus saying to you in each passage? What is he calling you to do or change? In Ezra 7:10, we see that Ezra set himself to study the law, then do it, *then* teach it in Israel. He studied first, then applied the Word to his own life before he taught the passage. Ezra is the example for us to follow as we prepare and lead Bible studies. Study first, then apply it to your own life, then teach it. In this way the passage will have gripped your own heart and life and you can teach it with real power and conviction.

- Don't consult a commentary, Bible study guide, or expert until you have completed the study yourself. After completing the study, it might be helpful for you to check your main interpretations with a trusted Christian friend, a pastor, an evangelical commentary or a Bible study guide.

- Don't preach, don't lecture, and don't share everything you learned as you prepared the passage. Get the group to discover and share what they observed.

- Encourage those who are sharing a lot to talk a little less and let others share, and encourage those who are not speaking up to share a simple observation that they see in the text.

- Colored pens or markers will help your group as they study the manuscript text. They can mark connections like repetitions and contrasts with different colors and see them better. They can mark themes. You may want to bring along a set or two of colored pens or markers for your group to use during the studies.

- There is a special small group leader resource area on the InterVarsity website at <http://www.gospelcom.net/ivpress/smallgroups/>. You can download helpful resources from this part of the website.

- Pray for the members of your group. Pray that they will be open to God's voice. Pray that they will seek to hear from God in his Word. Pray that they will put themselves into the study and that God would really speak to them as they dig into his Word together.

INDIVIDUAL OR GROUP EXERCISE

Try writing a lesson plan of your own for a group study of Mark 6:1-13. Then gather some friends and try leading it. There is a complete lesson plan for leading a study on this passage in appendix five. Consult this appendix only after you have created your own plan, and use it only to supplement what you have already done.

AFTERWORD

The specific method of Bible study explained in this book has been in wide use for the past three years or so. A number of regions of InterVarsity Christian Fellowship/USA use it as their basic Bible study approach. It was taught to more than fifty InterVarsity/USA staff and eighteen hundred student small group leaders at the Urbana 2000 Student Mission Convention in December 2000. It is used to train Christian believers in many countries of Eurasia and Africa to study the Bible. Students from Kiev in Ukraine to Omsk in Siberia are learning to study the Bible and are reporting great excitement. InterVarsity has also begun leading seminars in churches to teach laypeople to study God's Word in this way. In December of 2002 I helped lead a Bible study training seminar for an ethnically diverse group of about fifty laypeople in one of the fastest-growing churches in New York City.

We have gotten very positive responses. People say that they understand how to study the Bible for the first time in their lives; that they are meeting Jesus in his Word and hearing from him; that this method is bringing new life to their small group Bible studies; that they are sharing this method with their family and friends. All of this supports one of the basic convictions of this book: that studying the Bible with an open, seeking heart, depending on the Holy Spirit to lead you into all truth, and using a good contemporary method transforms lives and communities.

Here is a representative letter from a student in Washington, D.C., who was trained at the Urbana convention. I have edited out names, places and extraneous information.

I was one of the small group leaders at Urbana. That was the first time that I had ever been introduced to the communal discovery method of Bible study. I am also one of the freshmen girls' small group leaders at my university. So for our group study of John, we have switched over to this method. It is really good in that the girls love to be able to ask their own questions that they had about the passage and then help each other out by answering the questions. . . . The girls have done very well with picking out the important points. Sometimes it just seems overwhelming with so many awesome lessons to learn out of it. . . . I can really see God moving through us with this type of Bible study. The girls really love it and are much more open to talking and discussing with each other. It has been a time of growth and in-depth study in the Scripture since we got back.

In February of 2001 I had the great privilege of leading a team to a country in Africa to train the staff of the International Fellowship of Evangelical Students ministry in that country in this method of Bible study. Here is the report from one of the African staff:

There is nothing like it, Bob. Every week we encounter Jesus as we study Mark and our eyes are opened to his life and personality in ways that we can relate to. This is bringing consistent transformation in our lives. Praise. We pray that much more than this will happen to our students and participants come August.

I have organized a manuscript class in my living room every Sunday from 7 p.m. to about 9 p.m. I invite my neighbors and some friends to come for it. A student from one of our nearby campuses attended last Sunday and enjoyed it and promised to invite about ten of his fellow students. A mother of about your age, Bob, attended it two Sundays ago and invited another friend of hers. She is in charge of the teenage fellowship in her church. She plans to teach them. I praise God for the open doors.

More and more people and students are getting interested in manuscript Bible studies and I am trusting God to raise money to help in the photocopying of the clean copy for people.

Right now our national ministry adopted manuscript Bible studies for our national conference this August and has appointed me to be the organizer of it and train the trainers. All together we will have about 814 students to be trained (to be Bible study leaders) for the national conference, which we hope will be attended by 10,000 students.

Open-hearted, interactive, Spirit-led communal discovery Bible study not only transforms people, it is transforming the world.

APPENDIX 1

Sample Study of Mark 4:35-41

The first step is to enter the passage and observe it. Notice the details: *who:* Jesus "just as he was," the disciples, the crowd and the people in the "other boats"; *when:* evening of "that day"; *where:* going from one side of the lake to the other; *what* and *how:* a great storm, Jesus asleep in the stern of the boat, they call him "Teacher" and so on.

You might choose to relive the story as one of the disciples. First you would be terrified at the storm, then perhaps somewhat miffed that Jesus is asleep on a cushion while the boat is being swamped. You would hope Jesus would get up and help. But when he does get up, he doesn't just help—he calms the storm! You would be happy, of course, that you are saved, but in awe, wondering who your teacher really is. Is he more than just a teacher?

Next, generate some questions. Following are some you might ask.

1. What day does "on that day" refer to?

2. What lake were they near? Where is the "other side"? Where is the stern of a boat? What do we know about storms on the lake?

3. What does "just as he was" mean? Why would Jesus sleep during a storm?

4. What does "other boats were with him" mean?

5. What are the disciples' motives in waking Jesus up? How do they perceive Jesus at that point in the story?

6. What is Jesus' attitude toward the disciples when he wakes up?

7. After he calms the storm, why would Jesus ask them, "Why are you afraid?" Why would they still be afraid *after* he calms the storm?

8. What is "faith" for them at that point?

9. Why do they ask, "Who is this, that even the wind and the sea obey him?" What might that question reveal about their attitude?

Here are some possible answers to the questions, either from the text itself, the context, a Bible dictionary or map, or the Old Testament.

1. The context tells us that it was a long day of teaching for Jesus. He had told his most important parable, the parable of the soils; talked to his disciples about the secret of the kingdom; and told many more parables. So he would be tired.

2. These factual questions can be answered from the context, a Bible dictionary, an English dictionary and a map. The last place-name mentioned by Mark is Capernaum (2:1), which is on the northwest side of the Sea of Galilee. The story after this shows that they are going to the land of the Gerasenes, across the lake to the east. A dictionary tells us that the stern is the back of the boat. A Bible dictionary indicates that storms came up frequently on the Sea of Galilee, usually at night, often quickly and unexpectedly.

3. The context and the text itself clarify that "just as he was" means Jesus went into the boat after a whole day of teaching, so he would be tired. Mark is showing Jesus as a human being, just like us, who could be tired and sleep soundly even in a storm after a long day of giving himself to people.

4. The text shows that Mark might have included this detail to show that others were affected by this storm also and witnessed it, lending credence to his account. In witnessing the storm and then the calm, they too benefited from Jesus' power.

5. The text indicates that the disciples were desperate. They thought they were going to die. They needed everyone to help with bailing. And they expressed some annoyance at Jesus for not getting up earlier and helping. They call him "Teacher" because that was what he did all that day (we know that from the context). It seems that this was their perception, at that point, of who he was.

6. According to the Gospel of Mark up to this point, Jesus' goal was to train his disciples as fishers of people, makers of disciples and citizens of his kingdom. Their response to the crisis of the storm revealed their misunderstanding of who he was and their lack of trust in him. His attitude toward them and questions about their faith reflect his interest in probing where they were in their understanding of him.

7. According to a parallel passage in the Old Testament in Psalm 107:23-32, God raised up a fierce storm, the sailors were afraid, then God calmed the storm and they praised him. The fishermen on the boat with Jesus were Jewish men who knew the Old Testament, especially Psalms about sailors. Even if they didn't know this passage, they knew that only God can control the weather. Only God can calm storms.

   They woke Jesus up expecting him to help them. Instead of grabbing a bucket, he spoke to the wind and sea and calmed the storm! Putting all this together, they may have begun to realize that this person with them in the boat was more than a teacher. Could he be God, the God of the Old Testament? That thought would certainly cause shock, fear and questioning in their hearts.

8. Up to this point in the Gospel of Mark, Jesus had been teaching about faith—that it meant actively trusting him and following him, seeking him, believing that he was more than just a teacher. Thus, in the context of this story, faith is being in awe of Jesus; realizing that he is more than a teacher, that he is God; and actively trusting him to help them.

9. From the text itself, the context, and the Old Testament parallel, their question might be phrased as, "Who *is* this, that even the wind and sea obey him? Could this man, our teacher, asleep in our boat, really be God, the God of the Old Testament? Only God can calm storms, and he just calmed a powerful storm. Could it really be . . . ?"

Lindsay Olesberg summarizes Mark 4:35-41 as follows:

> After a full day of teaching, Jesus asks the disciples to row across the lake. A huge storm hits and the disciples are sent into the first crisis of the passage: "Are we gonna die?!" To make matters worse, Jesus sleeps through the emergency. After they wake him, he commands the wind and the sea to be still, and they obey him! Jesus' handling of the situation sends them into the second crisis of the passage: "So, who is this?!" Jesus is more than they expected. He isn't just a teacher; he is the creator of the whole universe. As the disciples discovered, following Jesus will lead people into situations that reveal the true state of their understanding of him. Jesus is using the storm in the disciples' lives to reveal their understanding of him and drive them to a deeper faith.

APPENDIX 2

Possible Application Questions from Mark 4:35-41

1. In what ways has Jesus been more than you expected? Praise him for this.

2. What storms are you experiencing in your life right now? How is Jesus using this to reveal the true state of your understanding of and trust in him? What is he trying to reveal to you about himself? What would "calm" look like for your storm?

3. We often lose sight of the reality that Jesus, whom we follow, is the creator of the whole universe. What areas of your life are you struggling to trust him in? In those areas, how does it make a difference to you to know that he controls creation?

4. Do you struggle more to believe in Jesus' care for you or in his power? Talk to him about those struggles and ask him to increase your faith.

5. On the back of your sheet, make three columns. Title them "Fear," "Stress" and "Distress." List areas of your life where you are currently experiencing any of those. How might Jesus work in and through these stressful situations to show his power and care for you?

6. In Psalm 107:23-32, those in distress because of the storm cried out to the Lord. The disciples accuse Jesus rather than ask for his deliverance. Are you more likely to accuse the Lord or pray when you hit difficulty? Give an example.

7. Spend time praying in pairs about the difficulties that you are currently experiencing.

APPENDIX 3

Sample Overview of Acts

Introductory Facts

- Acts was written by the physician Luke, author of the Gospel of Luke.
- The *New Bible Dictionary* has a good discussion about the three possible times when it could have been written, settling on about A.D. 70. It was written to a Roman audience.
- The *NBD* says that much of the factual information contained in Acts has been confirmed by modern archaeological finds.

What did I see as I compared chapter 1:1-11 and chapter 28 as if I had never read the book before?

- Different place—Jerusalem in chapter 1, Malta and Rome in chapter 28
- Different people—Jesus and the disciples in chapter 1; Paul, the "Brothers" and Jewish leaders in chapter 28
- Theme of kingdom in both chapters (1:3, 6; 28:23, 31)
- Both have teaching by and about Jesus
- Jesus talked of power in chapter 1; in chapter 28, power is demonstrated by Paul

What might have happened between Acts 1 and Acts 28?

In chapter 1 Jesus predicted that his people would be witnesses to the ends of the earth. In chapter 28 they reach Rome. So his promise is fulfilled. Somehow this guy Paul has become a major player, and in chapter 28 it is *we* instead of *they*. Chapter 1 mentions the twelve disciples. Chapter 28 mentions a larger and more multinational, multiethnic community.

What were some of my impressions of the book? What stood out to me?

- The power of the Spirit
- The boldness of the disciples' preaching and its center in Jesus' resurrection
- That this is a continuation of Jesus' ministry: Acts 1:1 says that in his first book Luke described what Jesus *began* to do and to teach; this book is a description of what Jesus is *continuing* to do and teach through his new body, the church
- Parallels between Jesus' ministry and the ministry of the disciples in Acts: miracles (the lame walk, the dead are raised, the blind see, the poor have good news preached to them); persecution and trial before Caiaphas; Stephen's Christlike death; Paul's trial, and so on
- Crossing to Gentiles, another culture—a major theme, the heart of chapters 8—12; 15
- Peter 1—12, Paul 13—28
- Strategy: first preach in the synagogue, then the prayer meeting, then the hall, and so on
- Obedience of disciples
- Various creative forms of witness
- The community—their love and commitment; their witness comes out of community
- The basics throughout: Word, prayer, fellowship, witness, missions, discipling, racial and cultural reconciliation

What are some things I think I can get for my life from this book?

- I am starting a new ministry in Eurasia. I need to see how the Holy Spirit worked through the early disciples to start churches all over the world.
- I often feel defeated by sin. I need God's power! How was God's power manifest in the early disciples?
- What were the priorities of the early disciples?

How does the book seem to be organized? Around events, geography, people, time? What chapters can be most naturally grouped together? What four or five major groups of chapters did I find? Give a two- or three-word title to each group.

Acts is organized around geography. Jesus said in 1:8 that they would receive power and be his witnesses in Jerusalem, Judea and Samaria, and to the ends of the earth. Chapters 1—7 take place in Jerusalem, chapters 8—12 take place in Judea and Samaria, and beginning in chapter 13, Paul and his associates go out to the ends of the earth, finally ending up in Rome in chapter 28. So 1:8 is kind of an outline of the book.

Is there a verse that reveals the main theme?

Yes! Acts 1:8: "But you will receive power when the Holy Spirit has come upon you; and you will be my witnesses in Jerusalem, in all Judea and Samaria, and to the ends of the earth." Jesus fulfilled that promise through his people.

How would I state the main theme?

Jesus is continuing his ministry, in the power of the Spirit, through the witness of faithful people who trust and obey him, first in Jerusalem, then in Judea and Samaria, then to the ends of the earth, producing a worldwide, multiethnic, ever-expanding, Spirit-filled body of believers.

What methods of evangelism and witness do I see in Acts?

- Public preaching
- Bold proclamation of truth of Jesus, centered in his resurrection and his presence now
- House to house
- Witness of the community in their love for each other
- Apologetic preaching (chapter 17)
- Arguing from the Scriptures in the synagogue
- One on one
- Friendship
- Even in jail and other hard circumstances

- Across ethnic and cultural lines
- Miracles
- Acts of love for others
- Both aggressive "in-your-face" preaching and quiet love

What truths about God stand out to me?

- He is powerful.
- He has a plan.
- He takes the initiative.
- He works through people.
- He works through individuals and community.
- He wants his people to cross cultures and ethnic lines.
- He is still working; his power is still available.
- His plan cannot be stopped.
- He is holy.
- He is loving.
- He calls for obedience, death to self.
- His call to die to self yields fruit and joy.

How do I apply this to my life?

The believers in Acts were really bold. They knew they were filled with God's Spirit. They knew God was working through them. So they stood up to opposition and were bold in their witness for Jesus. I need to be more courageous. I know I have God's Spirit in me, but I still hesitate to start conversations about the gospel. I have a trip coming up. I will pray that the Lord gives me a chance to talk to someone on a plane with me, and that I have the boldness to share with them about Jesus.

APPENDIX 4

A Manuscript Sample from Mark 1

Repeated Words:
immediately
and
gospel
wilderness

wilderness: Place of challenge
between God and humanity.

What is the gospel?
Isaiah 52:7

conflation
of Malachi 3:1
and Isaiah 40:3

The beginning of the gospel of Jesus Christ, the Son of God. As it is written in
Isaiah the prophet: "Behold, I send my messenger ahead of you, who will
prepare your way; the voice of one crying in the wilderness, make ready the
way of the lord, make his paths straight." John the Baptist appeared in the

Repent: Change
your mind,
attitude,
viewpoint

5 wilderness preaching a baptism of repentance for the forgiveness of sins. And
all the country of Judea was going out to him, and all the people of Jerusalem;
and they were being baptized by him in the Jordan River, confessing their sins.

(2 Kings 1:8)

John was clothed with camel's hair and wore a leather belt around his waist,
and his diet was locusts and wild honey. And he was preaching, and saying,

John was mighty -
but...

sandals: very
earthy, human
illustration

10 "After me One is coming who is mightier than I, and I am not fit to stoop
down and untie the thong of His sandals. I baptized you with water; but He
will baptize you with the Holy Spirit." In those days Jesus came from Nazareth

Why was
Jesus baptized?

conflation
of Psalm 2:7 and
Isaiah 42:1

in Galilee and was baptized by John in the Jordan. Immediately coming up out
of the water, He saw the heavens opening, and the Spirit like a dove

dove: same
word used for
sacrificial
dove p 28

word "immediately"
occurs 41 times
in Mark

15 descending upon Him; and a voice came out of the heavens: "You are My
beloved Son, in You I am well-pleased." Immediately the Spirit impelled Him
to go out into the wilderness. And He was in the wilderness forty days being
tempted by Satan; and He was with the wild beasts, and the angels were
ministering to Him. Now after John had been taken into custody, Jesus came

20 into Galilee, preaching the gospel of God, and saying, "The time is fulfilled,
and the kingdom of God is at hand; repent and believe in the gospel."

APPENDIX 5

Sample Lesson Plan for Communal Manuscript Study

The key to this study is to have the group generate questions based on and flowing out of the text, then spend the bulk of the time answering the questions together. In this way you interpret the text as a group. Then the teacher summarizes the main points and leads the group in processing or applying the passage. This lesson plan provides one hour of group discussion of Mark 6:1-13.

These notes are only *suggestions*. It is very important that you develop your own study and practice it before leading it.

Introduction (1 minute)

Context: In Mark 3:13-18 Jesus had appointed the twelve disciples to be "with him, and to be sent out to proclaim the message." The Twelve follow him and see him teach with power and perform great miracles. Our passage comes after a series of stories dealing with fear, faith and the authority of Jesus.

Creative idea for entering the text: Pretend you are a disciple writing in your journal before you go out (after Jesus' instructions but before you actually go). What are you feeling and anticipating? What questions would you have? Alternatively, you could review three ways to enter a text:

- Find the specifics by answering the "newspaper questions"—who, what, when, where, how?

- Find grammatical relationships or connections in the text. Are there words or phrases that repeat, are similar, or contrast? A cause that leads to an effect?

- Put yourself emotionally into the story. Become a character in the story. What are you seeing, feeling, smelling, experiencing?

Prayer and Individual Study (5 minutes)

Pray together, then give the group members time for personal study with the manuscript page, using the ideas for entering the text you have just told them. Instruct them to write down questions they might have: "As you are reading and studying the passage, write down any questions you may have that jump out at you from the text. Is there anything that interests or intrigues you? Anything you don't understand?"

Share Observations and Questions Together (15 minutes)

Note the questions as they are shared, but don't work at answering them yet. Keep this part lively.

Answer Questions Together (24 minutes)

This is the heart of the study. Break the group into smaller groups and have each group choose a question or two and work on answering it. Then walk through the passage again and as a group answer in sequence the main questions the group had. Work on answers together from the text. Here are some of the main questions they should come up with, along with some possible answers. Note that these are just *possible* answers. *You do not have to replicate these answers in your study.*

Question	Possible Answer
Why does Jesus send his disciples out two by two?	He is creating a community of witness and ministry, not just individuals. He sends them out "in community," by twos, so that they can support each other, encourage each other, and learn to minister together as a team.
What are some of the meanings or implications of the "authority" that Jesus gives the disciples?	When Jesus called them in chapter 3 he gave them "authority" over unclean spirits. For the past few chapters in Mark, Jesus demonstrated his loving, serving authority over nature, sickness and the demonic. Now he sends his disciples out to follow in his way of ministry—humble, servant authority.

Question	Possible Answer
Why does Jesus tell them to take nothing for their journey?	He wants them to trust him and not depend on outward devices or the power of money. Also, they had to depend on the people they went to. They truly went as servants, dependent on God and even the people they were going to minister to.
If he sent them out with nothing, why does he tell them to take a staff and wear sandals?	Taking all of Jesus' instructions together in this passage, his disciples actually looked like prophets or, even more so, shepherds. The staff was the basic tool and sign of a shepherd (see Psalm 23:4).
Why the emphasis on staying in one place?	This would help the disciples see who was for them and who was against them. Also, the disciples would have the time to "disciple" (to invest in) the people they were staying with. Finally, there was the practical advantage of everyone in the town knowing where to find the disciples so they could come and talk to them.
Why the emphasis on shaking the dust off their feet against people who do not welcome the disciples?	The disciples were to deal with the rejection by showing that the people were really rejecting God and incurring God's judgment. Also, in giving this instruction Jesus was preparing his disciples for the fact that many would reject them and their message.
What are some of the important things Mark is trying to teach by summarizing the way he did in the last two sentences?	The disciples "proclaimed that all should repent"— they preached the gospel verbally. They "cast out many demons"—they helped people spiritually. They "anointed with oil many who were sick and cured them"—they took care of people's physical needs. Total ministry to total people—their need for the gospel, their spiritual needs, and their physical needs.
What are the main points of tension in this story?	The tension, or the paradox, between Jesus' clothing his disciples with his authority while sending them out as poor, humble shepherds, dependent on God and even the people they minister to. He is actually creating little versions of himself, "little Jesuses," to go and minister.

Summarize (5 minutes)

Jesus called the Twelve to himself in chapter 3. Now he sends them out two by two to minister, but in such a strange way. He gives them his authority, the authority of God himself, yet he sends them out looking like poor shepherds, completely dependent on God and on the people to whom they are going. He tells them to take advantage of the hospitality system of the time and stay with people who will welcome them. They do go out, and they perform a threefold ministry—preaching the gospel verbally, helping people spiritually, and ministering to physical needs with God's power. They are "little Jesuses!"

Process and Apply (10 minutes)

Don't skimp on this time. Some possible application questions follow. Choose no more than two, keeping in mind where God has been leading the group as they have discovered the main points of the passage.

- What would it look like for you to minister like Jesus? How can you appropriate his authority and power? How can you care for others with his humility?

- Think through your daily life and ask yourself whether there is anything that you really do by faith. What are you really depending on God for? What in your life would collapse if God did not come through for you?

- Think about your fellowship group or church. How are you as a group reflecting Jesus' priorities in ministry? How are you as a group embodying his power and humility as you minister to others?

- How are you as an individual or a group preaching the gospel verbally to those who need to hear? How are you caring for people's spiritual needs for growth and wholeness? How are you caring for their physical needs?

APPENDIX 6

A Further Word on Commentaries

Most people, when they study a passage of the Bible, run first to a commentary for "answers," for insight into the meaning of the text. In a number of places in this book I have warned against checking a commentary first, encouraging you not to check one until you have completed your entire personal study of a passage. But once you have finished your study of the passage, you might want to go to a good commentary to check your interpretation against the interpretation of a scholar. This is another good safeguard for your Bible study. Just remember that even great commentary writers are only offering their human opinions of what the text means—educated opinions, but opinions nevertheless. The commentary is not the Bible.

You will need to check who the author of the commentary is, what kind of commentary it is, and what the author's approach to the text is. You are looking for a commentary by a scholar who actually deals with the text as it is and provides valuable insights and background information. Some critical scholars write commentaries that tear down the Bible. They don't really "receive" the text of the Bible as it stands, but instead try to reconstruct the text based on what they think the sources of the text are and what layers of writing produced the final text. They pick and choose, deciding that some parts of the text belong there, but some parts have been added to the text later and should not be there. In effect, this type of commentator reserves the right to decide what should be in the text of the Bible and what should not. They are putting themselves over the Bible as its judges, rather than putting themselves under the Bible and seeking to use their great knowledge and training to understand the text.

When I was in seminary I wrote an exegesis paper on Romans 13. I remember reading a commentator, a noted scholar and expert on Romans, who said that the solution to the "problem" of the meaning of Romans 13 is just to assume that Paul didn't write verse 5. Even though he had no historical, textual/critical or factual reason for taking verse 5 out of Romans 13, he did, and based his commentary on his reconstruction of what Paul "really" meant to write in Romans 13.

When using a commentary to get background information and to check the conclusions of your Bible study with an expert, make sure the commentary was really written by an expert, a trustworthy scholar, and not a devotional writer. Also, make sure the author takes the final text of the Bible as a given and comments on that.

In my opinion, the best single-volume commentary is the *New Bible Commentary* (IVP). The best commentary series is the New International Commentary series on the Old Testament and New Testament (Eerdmans). This series is rather expensive, however, and aimed more at pastors and teachers than laypeople. One of the best affordable commentary series for nonprofessionals is the IVP New Testament Commentary Series.

One of the most helpful new commentaries is a single volume that does not have the word *commentary* in it. It is a book published by IVP called *Hard Sayings of the Bible*. This book offers a very insightful and helpful commentary on verses in the Bible that are hard to understand, giving great insights into these confusing phrases or sentences. I highly recommend this book as an important aid to your Bible study.

BIBLIOGRAPHY

The Bible as God's Word

Packer, J. I. *"Fundamentalism" and the Word of God*. Grand Rapids: Eerdmans, 1984.

Sproul, R. C. *Knowing Scripture*. Downers Grove, Ill.: InterVarsity Press, 1977.

Stott, John. *The Authority of the Bible* (booklet). Downers Grove, Ill.: InterVarsity Press, 1974.

Vanhoozer, Kevin J. *Is There Meaning in This Text?* Grand Rapids, Mich: Zondervan, 1998. (Heavier reading than the others but deals with postmodern issues in a powerful way.)

Young, Edward J. *Thy Word Is Truth*. Philadelphia: Banner of Truth, 1990.

Postmodernism

Allen, Diogenes. "The End of the Modern World," *Christian Scholars Review* 22 (1989): 339-47.

Caple, Richard B. "The Learning Debate: A Historical Perspective," *Journal of College Student Development* 37, no. 2 (1996): 193-201.

Carson, D. A. *The Gagging of God*. Grand Rapids: Zondervan, 1996.

Cooper, R., and G. Buirrell. "Modernism, Postmodernism, and Organizational Analysis: An Introduction," *Organization Studies* 9, no.1 (1988): 91-112.

Fowler, James W. *Stages of Faith: The Psychology of Human Development and the Quest for Meaning*. San Francisco: HarperSanFrancisco, 1981.

Fryling, Robert A. "Being Faithful in This Generation: The Gospel and Student Culture at the End of the 20th Century." Paper delivered to the World Assembly of the International Fellowship of Evangelical Students, Nairobi, Kenya, 1995.

Grenz, Stanley. *A Primer on Postmodernism*. Grand Rapids: Eerdmans, 1998.

Long, Jimmy. *Generating Hope: A Strategy for Reaching the Postmodern Generation*. Downers Grove, Ill.: InterVarsity Press, 1997.

Longman, Tremper, III. "Reading the Bible Postmodernly." *Mars Hill Review*. Fall 1998.

Lynn, Steven. "A Passage into Critical Theory." *College English* 36, no. 3 (1990): 91-93.

Perry, William G., Jr. *Forms of Intellectual and Ethical Development in the College Years*. New York: Holt, Rinehart & Winston, 1969.

Tierney, William G., and Robert A. Rhoads. "Postmodern and Critical Theory in Higher Education: Implications for Research and Practice." In *Higher Education: Handbook of Theory and Research, Volume IX*. Edited by John C. Smart and William G. Tierney. New York: Agathon, 1993.

Unpublished Bible Study Resources Quoted in This Book

Conley, Sharon. *Manual for Communal Discovery Bible Study*. Unpublished manuscript, 2001.

Seiders, John, Bob Grahmann and Barbara Boyd. *Bible & Life Level II Teachers Manual*. Madison, Wis.: InterVarsity Christian Fellowship, 1997.

For further Bible study resources, see the websites <www.ivpress.com> and <www.ivcf.org>.

Scripture Index